WHITE, RED, AND BLACK
The Seventeenth-Century Virginian

Wesley Frank Craven is George Henry Davis '86 Professor of American History at Princeton University. His numerous publications include *The Dissolution of the Virginia Company, The Southern Colonies in the Seventeenth Century, 1607–1689,* and *The Colonies in Transition, 1660–1713.*

WHITE, RED, and BLACK

The Seventeenth-Century Virginian

Wesley Frank Craven

The Norton Library
W·W·NORTON & COMPANY·INC·
NEW YORK

First published in the Norton Library 1977
by arrangement with the University Press of Virginia

Books That Live
The Norton imprint on a book means that in the publisher's
estimation it is a book not for a single season but for the years.
W. W. Norton & Company, Inc.

Library of Congress Cataloging in Publication Data
Craven, Wesley Frank, 1905-
White, Red, and Black.
(The Norton Library)
Reprint of the ed. published by the University Press
of Virginia, Charlottesville, in series: Richard lectures
for 1970-71.
1. Virginia—History—Colonial period, ca. 1600-1775—
Addresses, essays, lectures. 2. Virginia—Emigration
and immigration—Addresses, essays, lectures. 3. Indians
of North America—Virginia—Addresses, essays, lectures.
4. Slavery in the United States—Virginia—Addresses,
essays, lectures. I. Title. II. Series: Richard lectures, University of Virginia, 1970-71.
F229.C897   1977   301.45'09755   77-9057
ISBN 0-393-00857-6 pbk.

1 2 3 4 5 6 7 8 9 0

PREFACE

IT WAS my privilege in the fall of 1970 to deliver the James W. Richard Lectures in History at the University of Virginia. The lectures are printed in the following pages, with only an occasional revision of the text, substantially as they originally were delivered, and in the style adopted for the purposes of an oral presentation. The special difficulty in much of the material employed will justify, I hope, the relatively heavy documentation that has been added.

In addition to the compliment that came with the invitation to deliver the lectures, I am indebted to the committee for the James W. Richard Lectures for suggesting the topic. I feel deeply obligated also for the many courtesies extended to me and my wife on the occasion of our visit to Charlottesville by the committee's chairman, Professor Neill H. Alford, Jr., of the School of Law, and by long-time friends in the Department of History. It would be difficult to find anywhere more gracious and considerate hosts.

Among the obligations incurred while preparing for the lectures, my chief indebtedness is to George Hritz and Michael Hassan, two able and faithful young men who in succession were assigned to me by the Bureau of Student Aid of Princeton University as research assistants. I am obliged to Lawrence Stone for several helpful suggestions, and to another colleague, Sheldon Hackney, for a critical reading of parts of the text, but such mistakes as may be found in it are wholly my own. My special indebtedness to Robert Brenner of the University of California, Los Angeles, is acknowledged in more than one place in the text. I am grateful to him for permission to draw upon his as yet unpublished

manuscript. At the Virginia State Library in Richmond I
am indebted to Randolph W. Church, State Librarian, and
especially to John Dudley for his friendly generosity in
drawing upon an unrivaled knowledge of the Library's rich
resources for the assistance of a visiting historian.

WESLEY FRANK CRAVEN

Princeton, N.J.
June 20, 1971

CONTENTS

WHITE

STRICT regard for the Indian's undebatable claim to priority of settlement in Virginia would require that this first discussion be devoted to the Red Virginian. But so largely do we depend for our knowledge of the area's original inhabitants upon evidence recorded by the white settler that it is helpful to speak first of him.

Who was he? No other question has more persistently claimed the attention of historians writing of the colony's early history, and no other has generated more controversy. Although the answer must be sought in records so incomplete, or otherwise uncertain in character, as virtually to guarantee the continuance of some very old disputes, it fortunately is possible to renew the discussion with several points on which a general agreement is possible.

First, he was, with no more than the rarest of exceptions, an Englishman. Convention requires that we pause here to acknowledge the presence of a few Germans, Poles, Italians, Hollanders, and Frenchmen, and of a larger but still small number of Scottish and Irish settlers, to whom must be added an indeterminate number of Welshmen. But no more than a pause is needed. The largest recorded migration of Scotsmen is that of 150 prisoners of war transported to the colony early in the 1650s, after the defeat of Charles II at Worcester.[1] Others migrated as individuals, among them the Reverend James Blair, the cantankerous first president of the College of William and Mary, and the Reverend Alexander Moray, who reported in 1665 that Scotsmen met intense prejudice in Virginia.[2] Only after the Act of Union in 1707 had created the United Kingdom, and the somewhat later rise of Glasgow to leadership in the tobacco trade, was the way cleared for a numerically significant migration from Scotland to the Chesapeake. The so-called Scotch-Irish migration from Northern Ireland belongs, of course, almost entirely to the eighteenth century. Irish prisoners of war shipped over in Cromwell's time may have outnumbered the Scottish prisoners. Moreover, Ireland quickly became a favored recruiting ground for indentured servants, and English shipmasters frequently found there an easy port of call for the purpose of rounding out their cargoes of servants on voyages to America. But there is good reason for believing that most of the Irish servants were shipped to the West Indies.[3] As for the Welsh, although many Welsh names may be found in the records of seventeenth-century Virginia, many of these can also be English. Firm evidence on the scale of the migration from Wales is extraordinarily difficult to find, even though there can be little doubt that the migration deserves special mention.[4]

To say that the early settlers of Virginia were predominantly English in origin is to suggest much that is of importance for an understanding of them. It is hardly necessary to dwell once more upon the great significance of their identification with the traditions of the Common Law, a decentralized system of local administration, and parliamentary usages of government for the development of the colony's political institutions. But it may be helpful in passing to observe that the especially active interest historians have taken of late in the study of English society at that time has called into question many of the assumptions upon which students of colonial America long have depended. If I may attempt the briefest of summaries, it appears that England at the time of our first settlements was not quite so staid, so fixed in the older ways of life, as we often have found it convenient to assume. Although the colonists came from an old society, one properly described as traditional, it was also a society that was experiencing a great deal of dynamic change. Many Englishmen still lived and died where they were born, but many others, and not just the rogues and vagabonds, were on the move from place to place—so much so that the decision to migrate to America must have involved, for some at least, much less of an uprooting than we long have imagined.[5]

General agreement can be had also on the relative un-importance, for the purposes of a discussion of the seven-teenth-century Virginian, of the migration to the colony during its earlier years. Although something like six thou-sand persons migrated to Virginia between 1607 and the dissolution of the Virginia Company in 1624, a census taken early in the following year showed hardly more than twelve hundred of them still living in the colony.[6] Some had come, in the first instance, for no more than a temporary and hope-fully profitable adventure. Of those who had migrated with a view to taking up a permanent residence, some had re-turned to England in bitter disappointment and a much larger number had died, more from epidemic disease than at the hands of hostile Indians. The population of Virginia at the close of the century was largely attributable to a much later migration. And this observation seems to be no less true of the great families which were rising by that time to posi-tions of leadership in a newly emerging society than of the common run of its members.[7]

Sharp differences of opinion once existed as to the English origins of these families, but again there appears now to be a general agreement. Certainly I could add little to what has been said on the subject by such modern scholars as Thomas J. Wertenbaker, Louis B. Wright, Peter Laslett, Bernard Bailyn, and Richard L. Morton.[8] In some instances it is pos-sible to speak with reasonable assurance regarding the men who founded the great families, in others the founder re-mains a person of obscure background. It is evident that the mercantile communities of England, especially London and Bristol, were well represented, as were also armigerous fam-ilies of the English countryside, usually by a younger son presumably ambitious to live in America on a scale com-

parable to that enjoyed by his oldest brother under the generally prevailing rule of primogeniture for the inheritance
of the family's estate. Very often, it appears, this younger son
may first have sought his fortune in London. Whatever differences of status may have separated the founders of Virginia's "first families" in England, they were all adventurers
in the fullest sense of the term, men willing to gamble for
high stakes in the new world in the hope of enjoying whatever advantage might be gained according to the conventions of an old social order. They have been so closely
studied, by their descendants among others, that we are not
likely to know much more about them than we do know at
present. The register of an English parish, however complete, does not always provide a positive identification of the
persons named therein. Even when heraldric records are
available, it can be difficult to read them with certainty, for
it was a time when the College of Heralds was notoriously
accommodating in its adjustment to a growing demand for
evidence of a genteel status.[9]

Perhaps no settler in seventeenth-century Virginia has
been more intensively studied than Richard Lee, the founder
of one of Virginia's greatest families. It is known, and here
I follow the official historian of the Society of the Lees of
Virginia, that Richard came from a Shropshire family, and
close reasoning from evidence partly circumstantial has established a strong probability as to his parentage, but it is
not known where or when he was born, and no certain information has been discovered regarding his career before
he reached Virginia, probably in 1640 but possibly in 1639.[10]
Perhaps we all should relax in the confident assurance of a
member of the family association who some years back was
quoted as saying "the Lees of Virginia need no English
ancestry."[11]

One other area of agreement demands special attention,
for in this instance it is necessary to emphasize the disagree-
ment between those who have bothered to be informed on

the subject and those who persist in writing about it without regard for the information that is available in the works of modern scholars. So far as I know, no historian has ever challenged the proposition that the vast majority of the settlers in seventeenth-century Virginia, perhaps 75 percent or more of them, reached the colony under some form of contract, or indenture, for a period of service sufficiently long to meet the cost of their passage from England. The question of the social origins of the indentured servant, therefore, has always been one of critical importance, and for a long time one of the more persistent stereotypes of American history was allowed to serve as an answer. In this stereotype the indentured servant has been presented as a person recruited chiefly from the lower levels of English society, and especially from the class of laborers, whose lot at the time was far from being a happy one; as very often a criminal or at best a rogue or vagabond; and as an individual so young as to have been an easy victim of the more unscrupulous methods employed by the recruiting agents who served the shipmasters engaged in the tobacco trade with the Chesapeake. Little wonder that more than one author, usually without research or even wide reading, has considered an account of the servant trade of the seventeenth century an appropriate introduction to the history of the slave trade.

A number of influences helped to establish this stereotype, beginning with the complaints made by seventeenth-century masters regarding their servants, the kind of complaints that masters of servants presumably have made in all ages and places—in some instances, of course, justifiably. The stereotype owes its survival in part to the inclination of a democratic America to believe that the country consistently has had a special attraction for the downtrodden of the old world. No less important may have been the opportunity historians have provided for the lay investigator who discovers his own descent from a person landing in Virginia under an indenture to assume that his ancestor represents the exception serving to prove the general rule. Above all, the record of the migration to seventeenth-century Virginia has remained so incomplete that historians necessarily have leaned heavily upon the evidence provided by legislative and judicial actions in the colony, evidence that can be misleading as to the actual composition of the migration.

Unfortunately, the English government, having conceded to influential promoters of colonization a right to ignore normal restrictions on emigration from the kingdom, bothered to keep few records. It is significant that of those kept by authorities in England the most informative to survive for the guidance of modern students reflect an effort to correct the more obvious abuses to which the servant trade was subject. Of these the fullest is a registry of approximately ten thousand persons sailing from Bristol between 1654 and 1685 for the American plantations, of whom almost half gave their destination as Virginia. Another surviving fragment is a comparable register for the port of London in the years 1683–84.[12] The sources are very limited indeed, but they have served nevertheless to call into serious question the bias so often displayed by even the best informed of historians who continue to speak of indentured servitude, this last a term too closely identified with the institution of slavery to be really helpful.

For some time now informed historians have been agreed that all kinds of Englishmen, persons drawn from all classes except those at the very top, migrated to the colonies under some form of indenture. Abbot Smith in a study of criminal transportation has greatly reduced the possibility that there was a significantly large criminal element in the seventeenth-century migration to the colonies simply by demonstrating the administrative inefficiency which originally characterized a developing system of conditional pardons. His study leaves no doubt that many more criminals were shipped to Virginia in the eighteenth century than there were during the seventeenth.[13] He also has cast grave doubt upon much of the evidence used by earlier historians in support of exaggerated estimates of the number of servants who had been kidnapped, or "spirited" out of the country, as contemporaries were wont to say. His discussion of a difficult subject leads to the conclusion that "a very small proportion indeed" of the indentured servants "were carried away forcibly and entirely against their wills."[14] Although the limited action taken by government to correct abuses in the servant trade was not always effective, it is safe enough to conclude that most of those who migrated to Virginia as indentured servants did so willingly, however much they may have been misled in their expectations.

Such a conclusion is reinforced by fragmentary evidence suggesting that the indentured servants on average may not have been quite so young as we often have thought—that most of them were at least eighteen years of age, and that the common age for migrating could have been twenty or more. This is the indication provided by the London list of 1683–84, and it is amply supported by the ages given in lists of some 2,000 persons sailing from London for Virginia in 1635.[15] By my count, these lists show that more than half of the passengers, who ranged in age from fourteen weeks to sixty years, were in the age range of twenty to twenty-nine (1,081 out of 2,013), that less than a third of them (626) were under twenty, and that in this younger group better than half (341) were eighteen or nineteen years of age. Perhaps the special concern shown by the legislature and the courts for protection of the most vulnerable element of the servant population has misled us.

It is not necessary to argue that none of the servants were young, or that there were among them no convicts, or to dismiss the oft-quoted statement of the mayor of Bristol in 1662 that among those sailing from that port for the plantations were husbands fleeing their wives, runaway children and apprentices, and criminals one jump ahead of arrest.[16] What is needed is a more balanced view, some recognition that there were others who probably were more representative of the whole.

The most interesting evidence as to who these others may have been has been presented by Mildred Campbell, an especially well-informed student of migration from England to colonial America. Professor Campbell's analysis of the occupations listed for male servants sailing from Bristol for the plantations after 1654 shows that only about 10 percent of them were listed as laborers. The largest single group were yeomen and husbandmen, with the yeomen outnumbering the husbandmen, and the next largest group were artisans and tradesmen, who were outnumbered nearly two to one by the farmers. When the two largest groupings are combined, the ratio of the sum to the number of laborers is something like five to one. The London registry of 1683–84 reveals roughly the same ratio, but in this case skilled workers are more numerous than the farmers, and among the latter there are more husbandmen than yeomen.[17] Even when allowance is made for those who may have seized an opportunity on their way to America to lift their status a notch or two, the evidence is impressive, and especially for the indication it gives that the agricultural segment of England's population was heavily represented. No less interesting is Professor Campbell's comment that her investigation of persons migrating to the colonies in the eighteenth century has had comparable results.

Perhaps we would have understood the character of the migration to Virginia in the seventeenth century more readily had the institution of apprenticeship taken firmer root than it did in our society, for indentured service in the colonies was a direct development out of that institution. Service as an apprentice was for the seventeenth-century Englishman a familiar way into any number of trades and crafts, as also into certain professions and some of the greatest trading corporations of the day. To become an apprentice to a Virginia planter, at a time when it was commonly understood that every occupation had its own mysteries and that they were best learned through the instruction of those who previously had been initiated, was a natural decision to make. To the validity of this proposition more than one surviving indenture testifies by its very phrasing. Thus, in 1659 Bartholomew Clarke was bound "apprentice unto Edward Rowzie of Virginia, planter" for a term of four years in return for the promise that he would be taught "the mystery, art, and occupation of a planter."[18]

Perhaps also the stereotype would be easier to correct if historians would stop speaking of the indentured servant as though he had been a commodity instead of a person. Rightly recognizing that his opportunity to migrate to Virginia depended upon the need for additional cargo on the outward voyages of the tobacco fleet, historians have talked not so much in terms of a migration as rather of an exchange of tobacco for labor. Not only have we thereby reduced the servant to the status of a commodity, but the emphasis given this exchange has helped to persuade us that the colony's labor force was annually renewed at a more or less constant rate through much of the century. That assumption, in turn, has led us to make estimates of the total migration to seventeenth-century Virginia which run as high as one hundred thousand or even more persons.

Now these, of course, are important assumptions, assumptions which unavoidably color any interpretation of the colony's early history, so much so as to demand the closest examination of any record that may be available for study. And there is one record, the only one that has any claim at all to comprehensive coverage, which has not been explored so fully as it might be, and which I now propose to explore.

It is the record provided by the land patents. It is well known that the distinguishing feature of Virginia's land policy to the end of the century was the award of a fifty-acre headright for any person brought into the colony, the award belonging to the person who paid the cost of the passage from England, including the person who paid his own way. Introduced in 1617 as a special inducement for adventurers in the Virginia Company's joint-stock funds to take up and develop the land dividends to which they were then entitled, the headright by a final revision of the company's policy in 1618 was limited to such individuals as might be sent to the colony before midsummer's day of 1625. For a decade after the company's dissolution in 1624 there was uncertainty as to the policy the colony would be allowed to follow, but in July 1634 the king responded to a fresh appeal from Jamestown by authorizing grants of land according to the rules previously established by the Virginia Company.[19] This clarification of policy was taken to mean chiefly that the colony's government might honor headrights for immigrants entering Virginia after midsummer 1625, and the ruling found immediate reflection in the issuance by acting Governor John West of some three hundred patents for more than two thousand headrights between the spring of 1635 and the end of 1636.* Through the following six decades relatively few land patents were granted upon other considerations than a claim to headrights. There were, it is true, other ways of getting land, including the purchase of previously developed properties by immigrants who had the funds needed for such a purchase, but it seems reasonable to assume that relatively few persons entered the colony without leaving some record of their entry in a land patent.[20] In any case, the land patents constitute the fullest record we possess of the migration to seventeenth-century Virginia, and I have concluded that this fact in itself might warrant an effort to subject the record to a somewhat closer analysis than has yet been attempted.[21]

Two main questions have shaped my investigation. First, I have hoped that I might establish some helpful indication as to the outside limit that should be placed on the size of the total migration to seventeenth-century Virginia. Second,

* See the table below, p. 15.

and more important, I have hoped that the data drawn from the patents might serve, however roughly, to distribute the migration over time, in such a way perhaps as to provide some better understanding of its essential character. The study has been made possible by Nell M. Nugent's *Cavaliers and Pioneers*, a publication containing abstracts of the Virginia land patents to 1666, and by the unpublished continuation of these abstracts that may be consulted in the Virginia State Library at Richmond.[22] These abstracts, which I have used for the years extending from 1635 through 1699, provide all the data needed for a quantitative analysis: the date of the patent in all but a very few instances, the name of the patentee or patentees, the acreage and its location, and the number of the headrights serving as a warrant for the grant. More often than not the persons providing the headrights are listed by name. Because the patents themselves quickly assumed a standard form, the tabulation of the data has been more tedious than difficult.

Let it be admitted at once that the data thus assembled can provide no precise answer to either of the two main questions I have raised. The abuses to which the colony's land system was subject are as obvious as they are well known. A claim to the headright might require no more than an oath taken in a county court before justices presumably favorable to the claimant.[23] Shipmasters took a leading role in speculative ventures involving both the headrights and the titles to land they served to establish. Sailors on service with the tobacco fleet might be entered as headrights for every visit they made to the colony.[24] That more than one grant might be made for the same headright is beyond dispute, and the problem of eliminating duplications defies solution because of the frequent repetition in the patents of the more common of English surnames and the unimaginative practice of seventeenth-century parents in designating their offspring by the more familiar of Christian names, and this without providing the child with a middle name. A further difficulty arises from the fact that the patents were grants for specified acreages previously located, and presumably surveyed; no close correlation can be assumed between the date of the patent and the time at which persons listed therein reached the colony. In all cases there would be some delay, and on occasion a very considerable one. But it is my impression that the normal delay could have been less than a year, or at the most not much more than a year, except for the period immediately following 1634, when some of the patents clearly represent a backlog of accumulated claims, and for the later years of the century, when the system was subjected to even more serious abuses than those I have mentioned.[25] In other words, there are reasons for believing that through much of the century, and for what proves to be the main bulk of the record, the land patents do provide a rough indication of the relative size of the migration in successive periods of time.

My own consideration of the corruptions to which the administration of the land system was subject has led me to one reasonably firm conclusion, which is that there could not have been more people migrating to Virginia in the seventeenth century than the total number of headrights appearing in the land patents of that century. Indeed, it is my strong suspicion that the migration actually was somewhat smaller than that total, but such a conclusion depends upon the answer to a further question. How complete is the surviving record? We must depend upon transcriptions from the original patents into the so-called patent books that were made by clerks who began their work late in the century. The very extent of the record surviving in these books has helped to persuade me that the loss to the ravages of time, to more than one fire at Jamestown, and to the carelessness of clerks in the secretary's office (so forcefully described by Robert Beverley in his *History*, written just after the century's close) probably was not very great, and that we have a reasonably full record.[26]

I am especially persuaded by internal evidence that the marked fluctuations I have found in the indicated size of the migration from time to time do not reflect serious losses in the record. The clerks made an obvious attempt in transcribing the patents to group them under the headings of the successive governors who made the grants, but one quickly learns in his tabulations that no main entry for an administration, or for a given year, can be regarded as complete. Later on, and in some instances very late on, one finds additional patents which the clerks evidently had turned up after closing a main entry, and which they proceeded to transcribe at whatever point in the book they had reached or wherever seemed convenient. It is reassuring when these later entries confirm, as they consistently do, the conclusion indicated by the main entry.

I readily agree that there are professional risks in the task I have undertaken, but possibly I can be viewed as of a sufficient age to assume them. Let me repeat that there is no other record of comparable fullness. It is a record historians repeatedly have drawn upon for other purposes. I found in its very existence a challenge I could not resist. However approximate may be the figures I have drawn from the land patents, they suggest a pattern in the migration to seventeenth-century Virginia which I hope may be considered significant.

A rough count of the headrights year by year, according to the year in which the patents were issued, indicates that there was no steady, annually recurring, or even steadily mounting or declining, migration into Virginia during that century. Instead, the migration appears to have achieved an impressive total by concentration in particular periods of time, and especially in the quarter century extending from about 1650 through 1674. By a rough count I mean that I have counted and tabulated the results of that counting, but I have not recounted. Nor have I attempted to correct the resulting totals by some reduction that might be considered a proper allowance for duplications or for other abuses in the administra-

tion of the system. It has seemed to me that any decision as
to the extent of such a reduction would be so arbitrary as to
offer no advantage over the simpler procedure of working
with the figures taken unchanged from the abstracts.[27]

The first period in which the land records suggest a heavy
concentration of immigration into Virginia embraces the
years extending from 1635 through 1639. The total number
of headrights recorded for those years, by my counting, was
6,766, for an average of almost 1,700 per year. These figures
can be misleading because more than a few of the headrights,
as I have previously observed, represented persons migrating
to the colony before, even much before, the year 1635. Obviously, the years following immediately upon the clarification of the king's policy in 1634 were a time for catching up
on a backlog of hitherto unconfirmed claims, or for recording
in regular form grants theretofore made by special order of
the governor and council. Perhaps the total is best read as
representative of the migration to the colony between 1625
and 1640, when the population has been estimated at about
eight thousand, an estimate that is reasonably consistent with
the figures I have given for the headrights in this period. It
is difficult to avoid the impression, however, that somewhere
around 1635 there occurred an acceleration in the rate of
migration from England, perhaps because the clarification
of land policy had provided a fresh encouragement.[28]

In 1640 the number of headrights recorded in land patents
dropped from the 1,262 of the preceding year to 278, and fell
in 1641 to 172. For 1642, the year in which Sir William
Berkeley became governor, recorded headrights show a pre-
cipitous rise to almost 1,300, but in the next year they drop
to less than 900, and in 1644 to 157, the lowest number I have
found for any year in the century. The annual average for
headrights confirmed in land patents issued from 1644
through 1647 is hardly more than 270, with the highest number (325) registered in 1646.

The years 1648–49, when the annual average rose to 600,

mark a distinct turning point that apparently reflects the beginning of an extraordinary migration which continued without significant break all the way through 1658. In the nine years extending from 1650, when over 1,900 headrights were recorded, to 1658, when the total number was better than 2,200, the grand total of headrights exceeded 18,000— for an annual average of over 2,000. The peak was reached in 1653, with almost 3,000 headrights, and the low year, with some 1,200, was 1655. The total declined in 1659 to just over 750 and dropped to just over 400 in 1660, but it began to pick up in 1661–62 at a rate providing for the four years an average of a little more than 750.*

In 1663 the total number of headrights jumped from the 947 of the preceding year to more than 2,400,† and in 1664 the highest peak for the entire century was reached, with better than 3,200 headrights. The total dropped in 1665 to a little more than 1,900, but rose in the next year to almost 3,000. And so it went for another eight years, with the 1,200 listed for 1671 being the lowest figure for any single year and the better than 2,500 for 1673 the highest. The twelve years beginning with 1663 and ending with 1674 show a combined total of 25,872 headrights, which is larger than the combined total for the remaining twenty-five years in the century. In 1675 the number of headrights recorded in land patents

* The count by year from 1635 to 1674 is as follows:

1635–		1645:	224	1655:	1,215	1665:	1,919
1636:	2,028	1646:	325	1656:	1,339	1666:	2,987
1637:	2,070	1647:	236	1657:	2,346	1667:	2,185
1638:	1,406	1648:	603	1658:	2,272	1668:	1,671
1639:	1,262	1649:	596	1659:	754	1669:	1,628
1640:	278	1650:	1,924	1660:	411	1670:	1,899
1641:	172	1651:	1,460	1661:	915	1671:	1,202
1642:	1,291	1652:	1,906	1662:	947	1672:	1,952
1643:	887	1653:	2,911	1663:	2,463	1673:	2,582
1644:	157	1654:	2,709	1664:	3,243	1674:	2,241

† Including patents granted by Berkeley for land in what became North Carolina. See note 25.

dropped from the some 2,200 of the preceding year to 709, a figure remarkably close to the average for this and the two succeeding years considered together. Only in 1678 did the total again exceed 1,000, and that level was next reached in 1682. The three years beginning then and ending with 1684 show an annual average just short of 1,400, which is also the approximate figure for 1687, but in all other years of that decade the totals fall well below a thousand. In the 1690s fluctuations were more marked than they had been at any time since the 1640s, and the annual average was 938.*

Now let me sum up. My tabulation indicates a grand total of more than 82,000 headrights listed in land patents during the years reaching from 1635 through 1699. Of this total, which probably should be viewed as substantially larger than the actual size of the migration for that period, well over half (almost 47,000) were recorded during the twenty-five years beginning with 1650. The total for the last quarter of the century was less than 24,000; for the years preceding 1650 less than 12,000.[29] Even if the estimated 6,000 persons migrating to the colony before 1625 be added, the indication remains that the great migration to Virginia had its beginning at mid-century and that well over half of those who migrated there during the whole course of the century did so in its third quarter.

The general conclusion to which these figures point, that the migration had an especially heavy concentration in the twenty-five years immediately following mid-century, is not in itself startling. This has been an accepted view for a long time, a view depending in part upon evidence roughly

* The count by year from 1675 through 1699 follows:

1675:	709	1681:	934	1688:	859	1694:	872
1676:	655	1682:	1,614	1689:	687	1695:	1,311
1677:	750	1683:	1,341			1696:	1,123
1678:	1,129	1684:	1,204	1690:	1,555	1697:	393
1679:	748	1685:	657	1691:	1,578	1698:	625
1680:	834	1686:	891	1692:	381	1699:	798
		1687:	1,380	1693:	752		

drawn from the land patents and even more perhaps upon the fact that the number of counties in the Virginia colony was exactly doubled in the two decades falling between 1648 and 1669.[30] But I, at least, found the extent of the indicated concentration surprising, and there are reasons for believing that the concentration may have been even more marked than my figures suggest. Since we are here primarily concerned with a migration of Englishmen, it should be noted that the total number of headrights includes over 4,000 Negroes, more than half of them recorded in the last quarter of the century and chiefly in its final decade.* It might be difficult to prove beyond dispute that the land records were progressively corrupted by abusive usages, and yet the weight of the evidence argues that this is true. Manning Voorhis, whose studies of land policy I have found to be especially well informed, has observed that the issuance of headright certificates increasingly became a routine formality handled by the clerks of the county courts and of the secretary's office at Jamestown, and that outright sale of headrights by the latter, for fees of one to five shillings per headright, began at some time before 1692, though it is impossible to determine just when or the actual extent of the practice. It is significant that when in 1699 the governor and council took formal action on the question of the illegal sale of headright certificates, they decided to continue the practice for the time being at the uniform rate of five shillings per headright.[31] That the development of this particular abuse was related to an actual decline in the migration to the colony is indicated by the fact that the fullest surviving English record of the migration, the previously mentioned list of persons sailing from Bristol, reached its end for all practical purposes in 1679. The editors of a published version of the list have explained its ending in the simple terms of a migration that had dried up at its source.[32]

---

* See below, pp. 85, 86.

Before turning to some further consideration of the implications of the data extracted from the land patents, let me
report on the opportunity I have had to check this evidence
against a recently published index of *The Early Settlers of
Maryland*, those who settled there by 1680, an index fortunately enjoying the sponsorship of the very capable staff
of the Hall of Records at Annapolis.[33] In more than one way
the migration to Maryland was an extension of that to Virginia, and the opportunity for comparison is all the more
welcome because in each colony the headright served as the
basis of its land policy. Perhaps it is more important to observe that the names in this Maryland publication are drawn
from land records which carry evidence as to the time of the
settlers' arrival in the colony, evidence that is wanting in the
Virginia patents. A sample drawn first from every tenth page
of a book running to more than five hundred pages, and then
from a comparable number of pages selected at random,
indicates that there were significant fluctuations in the size
of the migration to Maryland from year to year. A very low
level of migration through the 1640s is followed by an acceleration during the 1650s, and an impressive pickup after
1660, with the figures for 1665 apparently representing the
heaviest migration in a single year, which is only a year later
than that indicated by the land patents for Virginia. Of a
possible total of 21,000 persons who settled in Maryland between 1633 and 1680 more than three-fourths seem to have
reached the colony after 1660. It should be added that an
apparent drop in the number of immigrants between 1679
and 1680 may well represent nothing more than a normal
fluctuation.

When one turns to the problem of explaining the pattern
the migration to Virginia seems to have assumed, he thinks
first of certain political developments. There can be no doubt
that the revolutionary crisis centering upon England's Civil
War provides the basic explanation for the sharp decline
that came with the 1640s. It was a time of trouble with the

Scots, of rebellion in Ireland, and finally of open warfare
between the adherents of the parliament and of the king, a
time when stoppages were placed against shipping intended
for overseas employment, and when the energies of the kingdom were turned inward in the search for a solution to its
own problems. The acceleration of the migration after 1649,
when Charles I was executed, invites renewed attention to
the desire of royalists to get out of a country then seemingly
destined to be ruled by Puritans, but the point has to be
made with due regard for the evidence that the migration
continued after the restoration of royal government in 1660,
and for some time in mounting force. Apparently there were
followers of Cromwell as anxious to get out of the kingdom
as the royalists before them had been, and there is evidence
enough to support the view, despite its failure to find emphasis in the popular tradition. Too often perhaps the severe
penalties imposed by Virginia's general assembly between
1660 and 1663 upon shipmasters who brought Quakers and
"other separatists" into the colony, and upon those who wor-
shipped outside the Anglican Church or refused to have their
children baptized, have been dismissed simply as an expres-
sion of a prejudice common to the age.[34]

At the end of what may be described perhaps as the great
migration to Virginia, the effect of Bacon's Rebellion seems
to be clearly enough marked out for our attention, though it
has to be observed that a sharp decline in the migration
apparently preceded the rebellion itself. One can only wonder at the failure of three successive Anglo-Dutch wars to
leave more of a mark in the record, unless it be assumed that
the sharp drop in the figures after 1674 reflects the influence
of the third of these wars. The figures for the last quarter of
the century carry more than one suggestion as to the possible influence of political developments in England, and
especially those which indicate an increased migration to
Virginia during the closing years of Charles II's reign, a time
which witnessed a decided increase in the migration from

England to Carolina and the beginning of the great Quaker migration to the Delaware. But on this general point perhaps enough has been said.

The most interesting possibility for a significant correlation with developments in the homeland has nothing whatsoever to do with politics, or with the religious issues that are so central to an understanding of the century's constitutional crises. It is found in a recent charting by W. G. Hoskins of English harvests from 1620 to the middle of the eighteenth century, a study which is a sequel to a similar charting of harvests extending back into the sixteenth century.[35] If attention may be limited here to the period of our immediate concern, Professor Hoskins's study shows that the decade of the 1630s brought only one good harvest instead of the normal four in ten. The first half of the 1640s saw a decided improvement, but the harvest of 1646 marked the beginning of a five-year run of bad harvests. Cromwell's years were generally years of bountiful harvests, but another run of five successive crop failures began in 1657. On the eve of the harvest of 1662, as Professor Hoskins points out, English farmers had experienced within the preceding decade and a half no less than ten crop failures, and in 1661 the price of bread reached its highest level for the entire period covered by his study. Improvement came with 1662, and the years extending from 1665 through 1672 saw seven good harvests out of eight, as did also the years reaching from 1683 through 1690. The record for the 1670s was mixed. In the final decade of the century English farmers once again had the hard luck of harvesting only one really good yield. The correlation is by no means exact, but certainly the ten crop failures at mid-century, in which each five-year succession immediately preceded an apparently decided acceleration in the migration to Virginia, deserves emphasis. If there be a question regarding the migration's continuance through years of plenty, it may be well to recall that American history affords more than one example of migrations sustained over a significant period of time by their own momentum.

It is difficult even to suggest the influence economic conditions in the colony may have had, except that the evidently marked decline of the migration after 1674 could reflect the hard times of which the colonists bitterly complained on the eve of Bacon's Rebellion. Nor is it easier to find an answer to the other side of the question, which is the effect of the migration upon the colony's economy. Normally an immigration of proportions at all comparable with that to Virginia at this time had a stimulating effect upon a colony's economy, as earlier in New England and later in Pennsylvania, but in the case of Virginia the evidence so far assembled points chiefly to three major crises in which the colonists struggled none too successfully with the problems arising from an overproduction of tobacco, first in 1639–40, next in the mid–1660s, and finally in 1682–83. The price of tobacco seems to have fluctuated throughout the period of the great migration, being better at its beginning than subsequently. Only in the later years of the century does it appear that the dominant trend turned upward.[36] It is conceivable, however, that historians depending heavily for their sources upon protests against the restrictions imposed by the Navigation Acts, and ever anxious to find an explanation for Bacon's Rebellion, have drawn a darker picture of economic conditions in Virginia through the third quarter of the century than is warranted.

Mention must be made of a flurry of promotional literature issued at mid-century which promised an early diversification of the colony's economy, and of the leadership taken in Virginia by such men as Sir William Berkeley or Edward Digges in experiments looking to the development of new staples.[37] It should be remembered that the extraordinary success attending the conversion to sugar in Barbados gave fresh stimulation to old hopes for the production of a wide

variety of profitable commodities in the plantations, and
that even in the West Indies there were men who quickly
identified the more hopeful of such prospects with the mainland, notably those to whom the original proposal for a
settlement in Carolina has been traced. Evidence that some
of Virginia's immigrants came from the West Indies or
Bermuda must also be noted, but there can be no doubt
that the migration owed its impressive size to the far larger
number who migrated directly from England.[38] And after all
is said, it was tobacco that made the migration possible. However depressed may have been the prices paid the planters,
the value of their annual crop for purposes of trade, in England or elsewhere, was high enough to bring to Virginia in
some years as many as eighty or more ships.[39] Students of
other great migrations to America frequently have discovered
that the opportunity to migrate, to find a ready passage across
the Atlantic, can be the critical factor, and so it was with the
great migration to Virginia.

A recent doctoral dissertation submitted at Princeton by
Robert Brenner has substantially extended our knowledge
of the men who at mid-century held the lead in the trade
with Virginia as with other colonies.[40] He has described
them aptly as the "new merchants," for they had been quite
literally pioneers in the development of a new branch of
England's overseas trade. The opportunity they seized depended not only upon the expanding number of colonizing
ventures after 1624, but also upon the marked indifference
to that opportunity of the great merchants of London, those
holding membership in the corporations controlling the trade
with such areas as Moscovy, the Levant, or the East Indies.
The city's mercantile establishment, of course, had been significantly represented (especially by Sir Thomas Smith) in
the initial efforts to establish a colony in Virginia, but the
experience seems to have taught most of its members to avoid
such ventures thereafter.

The new merchants were for the most part men of obscure

origins. Perhaps the point that most needs to be made is that
some of the more successful of them enjoyed the advantage
of a firsthand acquaintance with the colonies, either as shipmasters or as actual settlers. Thus, Maurice Thompson, who
by 1650 had become the most influential of the new merchants, evidently went first to Virginia in 1617, possibly as
a shipmaster. His close associate and brother-in-law, William
Tucker, had migrated to Virginia as early as 1610. He sat
as a burgess in the first assembly of 1619, became a member
of the council in 1623, and in the census of 1625 showed a
muster on his property in Elizabeth City of eighteen persons
in addition to his wife and child.[41] Among the eighteen were
three younger brothers of Thompson who had come over
with Mrs. Tucker in 1623. Tucker remained active in the
affairs of the colony well into the 1630s and in 1636 he and
his brother-in-law were among the associates who purchased
the very considerable property of Berkeley Hundred.[42] Ultimately, he transferred his residence to London, where he was
living at the time of the Civil War. In reading Professor
Brenner's study one thinks ahead to the business relationship
between John Jeffreys of London and Richard Lee of Virginia, or the history of the Carey family, first of Bristol, then
of London, and later of London and Virginia.[43]

The newly developing trade with the colonies was a free
trade, in the sense that there was no corporate control for
the purpose of restricting participation, which became
widespread. Merchants of many different port cities had a
part in it, but from the beginning until past the end of the
century London held the dominant position. The point requires emphasis because some writers have assumed that at
least in the trade with Virginia Bristol held the lead at mid-
century, an assumption supported neither by the concrete
evidence we have as to the size of the migration from that
port to Virginia, which certainly was a small part of the
whole, nor by such records of tobacco imports into England
as have survived.[44] The point deserves emphasis also be-

cause it has a bearing on the question of the geographical areas in England from which Virginia drew its original population. On this question, the fullest evidence is once again that provided in the record kept by Bristol, and this shows that all sections of England were represented among the emigrants sailing for the plantations from that port, but that by far the larger part of them were westcountrymen.[45] Given this indication of the influence of proximity to the port of embarkation and London's leadership in the trade with the Chesapeake, it seems safe enough to conclude that although emigrants to Virginia might hail from any county in the kingdom, most of them came either from London or the so-called home counties lying immediately in its neighborhood.[46] It may be worth adding that Hugh Jones in 1724 described the speech of the Virginia colonists as being the speech of London.[47]

Both Professor Brenner and the late Richard Pares have demonstrated that the merchants trading with the colonies did not limit their activity merely to trade. Engaged in a trade that was basically one of supply and that repeatedly involved extensions of credit, they might find it a natural development of their interest to become promoters of settlement by providing a settler, or prospective settler, with a needed stake on some form of partnership agreement. Although the terms of such agreements varied, the mutual advantages remained much the same. The planter received a supply of servants, provisions, equipment, and perhaps land well beyond what his own means could have provided; the merchant assured himself of a right to market an increased share of the colony's crop and gained a measure of protection against what Professor Pares has described as "the chief risk in all colonial enterprise" by making his agent in the colony a partner.[48] Until further research has been undertaken, it is impossible to say how much this kind of promotional effort may have been involved in the great acceleration of the mi-

gration to Virginia at mid-century.[49] But it can be added that
by 1650 a number of Professor Brenner's "new merchants"
had won their way to positions of great influence and power.
It has long been known, of course, that Maurice Thompson
had a major role in the enactment of the Navigation Acts,
both those of Cromwell and the act which followed in 1660.[50]

Now, if it can be agreed, as I think it should be, that the
migration to seventeenth-century Virginia was much more
heavily concentrated in the third quarter of the century than
has formerly been believed, the implications for a reading of
the colony's early history are far-reaching indeed. Above
all, it has to be assumed that Virginia's population remained
until remarkably late in the century predominantly an immigrant population, and that only in the last quarter of the
century could a natural increase have begun to overtake
immigration as the dominant factor determining the size of
the population. Such is the conclusion that has to be reached
if in fact, as the data drawn from the land patents indicate,
the number of immigrants before 1650 was smaller than we
have thought, if the great migration which followed did not
reach its peak until well into the 1660s, and if the frequently
used contemporary estimates which place the population
in 1649 at fifteen thousand and at forty thousand in 1671
are anywhere near the fact.[51] It is impossible even to suggest
just when after 1675 the immigrant and native-born elements
of the population may have reached a balance, much less to
determine when the latter became the dominant element.
But the great size of the migration during the third quarter
of the century and the evidence of a marked decline in immigration thereafter, including evidence of the extraordinary
corruptions to which the land records then became subject,
argue that by 1700, or even before, most of the people living
in Virginia may have been born there.

I hope that these observations will not be considered ex-
cessively hedged about with reservations. The subject is a

difficult one and as yet has been little studied. It may be instructive to consider here the contrast between the estimated populations of Virginia and of New England at the end of the century. According to generally accepted estimates, the population of Virginia in 1700 was about sixty thousand, including Negroes, and that of New England ninety thousand, a total that would be higher if the descendants of the original Puritan settlers then living on Long Island and in East Jersey were included.[52] Even after estimates of the full migration to seventeenth-century Virginia have been reduced to bring them into closer accord with the evidence offered by the land patents, it seems possible that there were no more people living in the colony at the end of the century than had migrated there during its course, if as many. In contrast, the great Puritan migration of just over twenty thousand persons, which had ended not long after 1640 and apparently had not been followed by any numerically significant migration, was represented at the end of the century by a population some four times the size of the original migration.[53] The explanation for this contrast lies partly in a factor of time. In 1700 almost two full generations had passed since the end of the great Puritan migration, whereas in Virginia the time elapsed since the end of a much larger migration had yet to reach the standard allotment for a single generation.

But probably of much greater importance was a decided difference in the sex ratios of the two migrations. It is, of course, the number of females of childbearing age which determines in any population its potential for a natural growth, and on this question we have rather specific if incomplete information. Herbert Moller in a very useful study some years back concluded that in the original migration to New England the approximate ratio was three males for every two females.[54] In contrast, he found that the adult population of Virginia in 1625, as shown by the census of that year, had a sex ratio of almost four to one, that lists of over two thousand emigrants sailing from London for Virginia in 1635 revealed the even more adverse ratio of just above six to one, and that the registry of servants departing Bristol for Virginia after 1654 indicated a ratio of 308.3, which is to say a little more than three to one. My own test through a sample drawn from Nugent's *Cavaliers and Pioneers* indicates that the ratio for the full migration at mid-century could have been higher, but not so much so as to argue against the convenience of using here Moller's figures roughly translated into a ratio of three to one.* Such a ratio bespeaks a decided improvement since the earlier years of the century, but obviously the emphasis still belongs to a continuing imbalance of the sexes, so much so that it may be helpful to translate a three-to-one ratio into other terms. If the rough total of 47,000 headrights for the third quarter of the century can be used to determine the size of the overall migration to Virginia during that period, the number of females included in the migration at a ratio of three to one would have been less than 12,000. Given the nature of the record provided by the land patents, there probably were considerably less than 12,000 females migrating to Virginia at this time. Most of them presumably were of a childbearing age, but most of them also presumably were bound to a period of service that would postpone their prospects of marriage. Moreover, in 1674 many of them had only recently reached the colony.

How long the average delay of marriage may have been, or how far the delay's effect upon the size of the population may have been offset by illegitimate births, are questions that will have to be left to some student caught up by the current enthusiasm for demographic history and possessed of the courage to try his hand in the field of seventeenth-

* A sample of 4,272 headrights for white immigrants drawn from 72 different pages, selected at random and representing in time the years extending from 1648 to 1666, in Nugent's *Cavaliers and Pioneers* yielded the following results: 3,305 males, 967 females, for a ratio of 341.7.

century Virginia.[55] He will be faced by formidable difficulties, but whatever he can find will be most welcome. We
know practically nothing regarding such basic questions as
the age of marriage, size of family, or life expectancy in
seventeenth-century Virginia, and can only be warned by
studies of other areas—chiefly New England—which have
significantly modified assumptions historians long have regarded as dependable. Thus, the average age of marriage in
colonial America seems to have been younger than it was
in contemporary Europe, but not so young as tradition has
placed it. Similarly, the colonial family apparently was larger
than the average at that time in Europe, but not nearly so
large as we have often thought.[56] Although much attention
has been devoted to the extraordinary mortality suffered by
the earliest emigrants to Virginia, it remains impossible to
speak with certainty on the probable death rate among new
arrivals later in the century. Such evidence as we have argues
that the "seasoning" period, as the colonists described the
first year of adjustment, still could be difficult but usually
was not fatal.[57]

Until these and other fundamental questions have been
more fully explored, we presumably should restrain whatever impulse we may feel to talk of developments in the latter
half of the century in terms of what might be expected of a
second or third generation of Virginians. Presumably, too,
the statistics assembled by Philip Alexander Bruce to dem-
onstrate a high level of literacy among the colonists—high,
that is, by comparison with what is known of literacy in
contemporary England—speak less of the provisions made
for education in seventeenth-century Virginia than of the
educational advantages enjoyed by those who migrated there
at the time.[58] That social and political unrest should have
profoundly disturbed the colony during the last quarter of
the century need not surprise us, for the spectacular growth
Virginia recently had experienced hardly could have failed
to have its unsettling effects.

Perhaps the chief need is to place the great migration to Virginia in the context of the even greater migration from England to seventeenth-century America, beginning at Jamestown in 1607 and ending with the settlement of Pennsylvania as the century drew toward its close. Those who would understand its full history may well ask where in the middle of the seventeenth century an Englishman inclined to migrate to America could have readily gone? There was shipping enough to carry him to the West Indies, but there a rapid conversion to slave labor must have limited the prospect he saw. New England, disappointed in the failure of England, even of the English Puritans in their moment of triumph, to rally to the standard it had set, had adopted an exclusive attitude toward all but its own kind. New York, even after the English conquest, remained Dutch. The Carolina venture was extraordinarily slow to get off the ground, and its leaders at first had a very limited interest in encouraging a migration from England. There remain Virginia and its Chesapeake neighbor, Maryland.

In conclusion, let me return to the question posed at the beginning of this discussion. Who was this Englishman who migrated to Virginia, more often than not in the third quarter of the seventeenth century? If I have read the evidence correctly, he was young but not a child; he may have come from any part of England but in most instances probably from the southeastern section of the kingdom. His religious convictions might speak for any of the divergences of opinion that beset the English church in that century but in the act of migrating he belonged to no organized religious movement. As for his political opinions, he may have supported the king, he may have backed parliament, even Cromwell, or he may simply have displayed the ambivalence of attitude which so many men through the course of history have shown when living in the midst of a revolution. Certainly, he was rarely a zealot. Primarily, he was an adventurer, and in the fullest sense of the word, a man seeking the main chance for

himself in that part of the new world which at the moment
seemed to offer for him the best chance.

Notes

1. Philip Alexander Bruce, *Economic History of Virginia in the
Seventeenth Century* (New York, 1895), I, 609; Abbot Emerson Smith,
*Colonists in Bondage: White Servitude and Convict Labor in America,
1607–1776* (Chapel Hill, N.C., 1947), p. 156. French names are scattered
throughout the records, and some of them probably belonged to Hugue-
nots, but no Huguenot settlement was established before 1700. See
Richard L. Morton, *Colonial Virginia* (Chapel Hill, N.C., 1960), I, 367–68.

2. *William and Mary Quarterly*, 2d ser., II (1922), 157–61.

3. Smith, *Colonists in Bondage*, pp. 167, 172–74; Bruce, *Economic
History*, I, 609–10.

4. Thus the index for Smith's *Colonists in Bondage* carries only two
entries for Welsh migration, neither of them involving Virginia, and the
index for Edward G. Hartmann, *Americans from Wales* (Boston, 1967)
has no entry at all for Virginia. But see Mildred Campbell, "Social
Origins of Some Early Americans," in James M. Smith, *Seventeenth-
Century America: Essays in Colonial History* (Chapel Hill, N.C., 1959),
p. 78.

5. The bibliography is far too extensive for listing here, but among
recent studies of note are Lawrence Stone, *The Crisis of the Aristocracy,
1558–1641* (Oxford, 1965); Peter Laslett, *The World We Have Lost* (London, 1965); and Carl Bridenbaugh, *Vexed and Troubled Englishmen,
1590–1642* (New York, 1967).

6. To be specific, 1,232. For the census, see John Camden Hotten, *The
Original Lists of Persons of Quality . . . and Others Who Went from
Great Britain to the American Plantations, 1600–1700* (London, 1874),
pp. 201–65.

7. See especially Bernard Bailyn's discussion in "Politics and Social
Structure in Virginia," in J. M. Smith, *Seventeenth-Century America*,
pp. 90–115.

8. In addition to works previously cited and Wertenbaker's well-
known studies, see Louis B. Wright, *The First Gentlemen of Virginia*
(San Marino, Calif., 1940); and Peter Laslett, "The Gentry of Kent in
1640," *Cambridge Historical Journal*, IX (1947–49), 148–64.

9. Stone, *Crisis of the Aristocracy*, pp. 23, 49–77.

10. Ludwell Lee Montague, "Richard Lee, the Emigrant, 1613(?)–
1664," *Virginia Magazine of History and Biography*, LXII (1954), 3–49.

11. See the periodically issued publication of The Society of the Lees of Virginia for June 5, 1969.

12. For a published list of names taken from the Bristol registry, see N. Dermott Harding and Wm. D. Bowman, *Bristol and America: A Record of the First Settlers in the Colonies of North America, 1654–1685* (London, n.d.); and for a breakdown of the totals according to destination and year of departure, A. E. Smith, *Colonists in Bondage*, pp. 308–9, where details of the London list are also given.

13. A. E. Smith, *Colonists in Bondage*, pp. 89–135. His estimate of the total number of persons conditionally pardoned between 1661, when a reasonably full record has its beginning, and 1700 is approximately 4,500, and of this total many seem not to have been transported at all. Of those transported by no means all were sent to Virginia. On p. 361, n. 37, he comments that there is "no evidence whatever" that convicts were shipped to Virginia between 1670, when the colony prohibited their importation, and 1718, when new and more effective procedures were adopted. Authors inclined to exaggerate the number of convicts shipped before 1661 should read closely *ibid.*, pp. 92–96.

14. *Ibid.*, pp. 67–86, and this last page for the quotation.

15. Mildred Campbell reports that in the London list of 1683–84 the "majority were between the ages of eighteen and twenty-four, with twenty-one and twenty-two predominating." See J. M. Smith, *Seventeenth-Century America*, p. 74. The lists for 1635 are scattered in Hotten, *Original Lists*, between pp. 35–138. See also Bruce, *Economic History*, I, 600–601, for comment on the age level of servants in the census of 1625 which suggests that it could have been lower in the period of the company's control, and which was made with a view to discounting the size of the criminal element in the population at that time.

16. For the quotation, see A. E. Smith, *Colonists in Bondage*, pp. 82–83. It perhaps should be added that Mr. Smith himself arrived at a none too favorable view of the overall quality of the servants brought to the colonies (see *ibid.*, pp. 299–300).

17. In J. M. Smith, *Seventeenth-Century America*, pp. 71–72.

18. See Bruce, *Economic History*, II, 1n. It is worth noting that the Lords of Trade in 1676, while reviewing a statute of Jamaica "for the good governing of Christian servants," objected to the use therein of "the word *Servitude*, being a mark of bondage and slavery," and advised the use instead of "the word *Service* since these servants are only apprentices for years." *Calendar of State Papers, Colonial, 1675–1676*, p. 394.

19. Wesley Frank Craven, *The Southern Colonies in the Seventeenth Century, 1607–1689* (Baton Rouge, La., 1949), p. 128; *Calendar of State Papers, Colonial, 1574–1660*, p. 185; H. R. McIlwaine, *Minutes of the Council and General Court of Colonial Virginia, 1622–1632, 1670–1676* (Richmond, Va., 1924), p. 481.

20. See Bailyn, "Politics and Social Structure in Virginia." Among those purchasing a developed property was Nathaniel Bacon, the rebel, who

apparently secured no patent based upon headrights. Mention belongs also to the very considerable escheated properties that could be acquired through payment of the necessary fees. See Bruce, *Economic History*, I, 564–67, for discussion of the subject together with that of properties to which title had lapsed through failure to "seat" them.

21. Except for Thomas J. Wertenbaker, *The Planters of Colonial Virginia* (Princeton, N. J., 1922), the land records have been subjected to little analytical investigation, and he primarily was interested in demonstrating that the representative planter of seventeenth-century Virginia was a small farmer who not infrequently had first reached the colony as a servant. Bruce, of course, used the land patents very effectively in support of conclusions drawn also from a remarkably close study of the court records.

22. The full title of Mrs. Nugent's book is *Cavaliers and Pioneers: Abstracts of Virginia Land Patents and Grants, 1623–1800, Volume I, 1623–1666* (Richmond, 1934). Here are published abstracts for Patent Books 1 to 5; for the later years of the century I have used the unpublished abstracts from Patent Books 6 to 9 which hereafter are most conveniently cited by reference to the number of the Patent Book and the page of the volumes in which the abstracts have been bound. Perhaps it should be added that the figures drawn from Mrs. Nugent's volume indicate a migration considerably in excess of the "nearly" twenty five thousand names listed in George C. Greer, *Early Virginia Immigrants, 1623–1666* (Richmond, 1912). I am indebted to Mr. John Dudley of the Virginia State Library for the information that Mr. Greer's list does not in fact cover the full period claimed in the book's title.

23. See, for example, Stratton Nottingham, *Certificates and Rights, Accomack County, Virginia, 1663–1709* (Onancock, Va., 1929), or the "Order Book, 1678–1693" of the Henrico County Court, pp. 254–55.

24. The record must have been set by William Odeon, whose name was entered for sixteen headrights in a patent of 1690 (Patent Book 8, p. 347). Commonly, such duplicate entries would run between two and five or occasionally six.

25. See the evidence given below, pp. 90–91, for the Menefie and Scarborough patents of 1638 and 1656, and Montague's discussion in "Richard Lee, the Emigrant, 1613(?)–1664," of Lee's movements in 1650 in relationship to patents secured in 1651, one as early as May of that year. Notice also, in Mrs. Nugent's *Cavaliers and Pioneers*, pp. 425ff., the block of patents for land in what became North Carolina, all dated in September 1663, the year of the first Carolina charter. It is difficult to interpret this as representative of anything other than a concerted movement depending upon some agreement with the Carolina proprietors, among whom was Sir William Berkeley, in whose name the patents were issued in the regular form of a Virginia patent. One of the patentees was Thomas Woodward, who had received a commission as "sole surveyor of Carolina" from Berkeley in March 1663 and who two years later

was still in office. McIlwaine, *Minutes of the Council and General Court,* p. 507; Craven, *Southern Colonies,* p. 327.

26. In the burning of Jamestown by Bacon in 1676, the official records were removed from the statehouse to a place of safekeeping by William Drummond. See Morton, *Colonial Virginia,* I, 270. For Beverley's account, see *The History and Present State of Virginia,* ed. Louis B. Wright, (Chapel Hill, N.C., 1947), pp. 102–3, where Beverley tells of the fire of October 1698 which ultimately led the government to move to Williamsburg, and then credits Sir Edmund Andros with causing "all the Records, and Papers, which had been sav'd from the Fire, to be sorted again, and register'd in Order, and indeed in much better Order, than ever they had been before." Beverley himself served as clerk in the secretary's office in the 1690s, and so his strictures on the earlier conduct of the office, incidentally limited to the period after Bacon's Rebellion, may have been more severe than was deserved.

27. One exception to this statement should be noted. Where I have noticed the kind of duplication mentioned above in n. 24, I have reduced the number to a single headright, on the assumption that some of the sailors may actually have taken residence in the colony. Perhaps it should be added that a number of patents granted after the Restoration as renewals of grants received in Cromwell's time are not represented in the figures which follow. See Nugent's note on p. 412 of *Cavaliers and Pioneers.*

28. And not only because of the previously mentioned 2,000 persons sailing from London in that year for Virginia. Governor Harvey reported in 1630 a population of 2,500, which is a figure much to be preferred over an earlier estimate of 3,000 in 1628, if only because of the known tendency toward exaggeration in all such estimates. A census taken early in 1635 indicates that the population had been approximately doubled since 1630, and a report of the census stated that after it had been completed 205 persons had arrived from Bermuda. Evarts B. Greene and Virginia Harrington, *American Population before the Federal Census of 1790* (New York, 1932), p. 136; Bruce, *Economic History,* I, 319–20; *Calendar of State Papers, Colonial, 1574–1660,* pp. 201, 208.

29. With regard to the figures for the last quarter of the century, it probably should be noted that the Jamestown government evidently made no headright grants in the Northern Neck after 1677, when Lord Culpeper, its proprietor, succeeded to the governorship. See [Fairfax Harrison], *Landmarks of Old Prince William* (Richmond, 1924), p. 194. Although from that year forward the proprietorship was represented in the colony by resident agents, its land office was not opened until the 1690s, and its affairs remained ensnarled in a bitter contest with the inhabitants of the area, and with the colony's government, until near the close of the century. During that interval, it seems doubtful that there was any large migration into the area. See in addition, [Fairfax Har-

rison], *Virginia Land Grants* (Richmond, 1925); and Richard Beale
Davis, *William Fitzhugh and His Chesapeake World, 1676–1701* (Chapel
Hill, N.C., 1963), pp. 39–45.

30. In fixing the origin of Middlesex County in 1669, I follow the
argument of Floyd W. Sydnor, "Middlesex County, Virginia: The Date
of Its Origins," *Virginia Magazine of History and Biography*, XLII
(1934), 28–33.

31. Manning C. Voorhis, "The Land Grant Policy of Colonial Virginia, 1607–1774" (Ph.D. diss., University of Virginia, 1940), pp. 30–86
especially; and his "Crown *versus* Council in the Virginia Land Policy,"
William and Mary Quarterly, 3d ser., III (1946), 499–514. See also Harrison's *Virginia Land Grants*, pp. 33–41, 125–27; and Bruce, *Economic
History*, I, 518–26, where the author leans heavily for documentation
of the more serious abuses upon Henry Hartwell, James Blair, and
Edward Chilton, *The Present State of Virginia and the College*, written in 1697 and first published at London in 1727.

32. Harding and Bowman, *Bristol and America*. Only a very few
scattered entries follow 1679, the last in 1685.

33. Gust Skordas, ed., *The Early Settlers of Maryland: An Index
to Names of Immigrants Compiled from Records of Land Patents, 1633–
1680, in the Hall of Records, Annapolis, Maryland* (Baltimore, 1968).

34. This legislation is most conveniently consulted in an appendix to
George M. Brydon, *Virginia's Mother Church* (Richmond, 1947), pp.
474–78. On the main point, see Beverley's *History* (first published in
1705), pp. 287–88, though he discounts the size of the "Roundhead"
migration. Mildred Campbell has suggested (J. M. Smith, *Seventeenth-
Century America*, pp. 86–89) that it was no mere chance that the largest
migration recorded at Bristol for a single year came in 1662, when the
first of the Restoration statutes for the suppression of religious dissent
went into effect, and when more than five hundred of the more than
eight hundred persons sailing that year from Bristol gave their destination as Virginia. See A. E. Smith, *Colonists in Bondage*, p. 309. A member of the House of Burgesses was expelled in 1663 for refusing the
oath of supremacy, and servant insurrections occurring at about the
same time were charged to the influence of Cromwellians, possibly for
good reason. See Brydon, *Virginia's Mother Church*, pp. 191–92, 197; and
Richard B. Morris, *Government and Labor in Early America* (New York,
1946), pp. 171–75. It may or may not be worth adding that this was the
period when the vestry, theretofore elected, became a closed and self-
perpetuating corporation, with the power to appoint churchwardens.

35. W. G. Hoskins, "Harvest Fluctuations and English Economic
History, 1620–1759," *Agricultural History Review*, XVI (1968), Pt. I,
15–31.

36. Lewis C. Gray, *History of Agriculture in the Southern United
States to 1860* (Washington, 1933), I, 259–68.

37. Craven, *Southern Colonies*, pp. 251–53, where several of these
tracts are cited.

38. A report in the 1660s that four thousand persons had migrated from Barbados to Virginia and Surinam between 1646 and 1658 leaves the size of the migration to either place very uncertain. See Vincent T. Harlow, *A History of Barbados, 1625–1685* (Oxford, 1926), p. 340, and for a later time Richard S. Dunn, "The Barbados Census of 1680," *William and Mary Quarterly*, 3d ser., XXVI (1969), pp. 26–30 especially. As for Bermuda the evidence is even more limited. See note 28 above.

39. Bruce, *Economic History*, I, 385.

40. Robert Paul Brenner, "Commercial Change and Political Conflict: The Merchant Community in Civil War London" (Ph.D. diss., Princeton University, 1970).

41. Hotten, *Original Lists*, p. 244.

42. Nugent, *Cavaliers and Pioneers*, p. 53.

43. See in addition to Montague, "Richard Lee, the Emigrant, 1613(?)–1664," Jacob M. Price, "Who Was John Norton?", *William and Mary Quarterly*, 3d ser. XIX (1962), 400–407.

44. These records, though fragmentary, indicate that normally imports by London were considerably larger than those for all the outports combined. See the figures compiled by Jacob M. Price for *Historical Statistics of the United States*, p. 766; his *The Tobacco Adventure to Russia*, in *Transactions of the American Philosophical Society*, n.s., Vol. 51, Pt. 1, (1961), 5; Neville Williams, "England's Tobacco Trade in the Reign of Charles I," *Virginia Magazine of History and Biography*, LXV (1957), 403–49; Stanley Gray and C. J. Wyckoff, "The International Tobacco Trade in the Seventeenth Century," *Southern Economic Journal*, VII (1940), 1–26.

45. Mildred Campbell in J. M. Smith, *Seventeenth-Century America*, pp. 78–79.

46. *Ibid.*, where Professor Campbell reports that the London list of 1683–84 shows that the emigrants came largely from London and Middlesex, but that Yorkshire had the next largest representation.

47. Hugh Jones, *The Present State of Virginia*, ed. Richard L. Morton (Chapel Hill, N.C., 1956), pp. 18, 80. On this last page, Jones wrote: "The Habits, Life, customs, computations, etc. of the Virginians are much the same as about London, which they esteem their home; and for the most part have contemptible notions of England, and wrong sentiments of Bristol, and the other outports, which they entertain from seeing and hearing the common dealers, sailors, and servants that come from those towns, and the country places in England and Scotland, whose language and manners are strange to them; for the planters, and even the native Negroes generally talk good English without idiom or tone. . . ."

48. Richard Pares, *Merchants and Planters*, published as *Economic History Review Supplement*, no. 4 (Cambridge, 1960), where on pp. 52–55 he includes a number of such partnership agreements with planters in the West Indies. For the quotation, see p. 5. See also Bridenbaugh, *Vexed and Troubled Englishmen*, pp. 426–27.

49. See Bruce, *Economic History*, II, 364, 379–80, for comment upon factors representing English merchants in the colony on terms of partnership, and upon the extensive properties held there by English merchants, at times in partnership with resident colonists.

50. Charles M. Andrews, *The Colonial Period of American History* (New Haven, 1934–38), IV, 54, 56, 63n.

51. Greene and Harrington, *American Population*, p. 136, where 1648 is wrongly substituted for 1649.

52. See *Historical Statistics of the United States, Colonial Times to 1957* (Washington, 1960), p. 756, and Beverley's *History*, p. 253.

53. The figure usually given for the Puritan migration is that of Edward Johnson: 21,200. For the most recent discussion, see Bridenbaugh, *Vexed and Troubled Englishmen*, pp. 467–73.

54. Herbert Moller, "Sex Composition and Correlated Culture Patterns of Colonial America," *William and Mary Quarterly*, 3d ser., II (1945), 113–53.

55. On both questions, of course, there are helpful indications. A not inconsiderable body of legislation, including provisions for the issuance of marriage licenses, testifies to the need for special protection of the master's right of property in a female servant. See Craven, *Southern Colonies*, pp. 273–74; Bruce, *Economic History*, II, 35–38; and for evidence that the problem of bastardy was serious, Bruce, *Institutional History of Virginia in the Seventeenth Century* (New York, 1910), I, 45–50, 83–85; and Arthur P. Scott, *Criminal Law in Colonial Virginia* (Chicago, 1930), pp. 279–81.

56. For example, Robert V. Wells, "A Demographic Analysis of Some Middle Colony Quaker Families of the Eighteenth Century" (Ph.D. diss., Princeton University, 1969) reports an average age at first marriage for women of 22.8 and 26.5 for men, and an average size for the family of 5.69 children.

57. Wyndham B. Blanton, *Medicine in Virginia in the Seventeenth Century* (Richmond, 1930), p. 39, for Berkeley's statement in 1671 that "there is not often unseasoned hands (as we term them) that die now."

58. Bruce, *Institutional History*, I, 450–59. To his evidence can be added a list of one hundred men in Northumberland County who in the spring of 1652, shortly after the colony's surrender to Cromwell, signed an engagement to support the Commonwealth of England, of whom fifty-three signed in full and forty-seven with their mark. See *Virginia Magazine of History and Biography*, XXXIX (1941), 33–36. There is an interesting opportunity for comparison with the record of some nine thousand men in different parts of England who in 1642 signed an oath affirming their loyalty to the parliamentary cause. From this evidence Lawrence Stone tentatively has concluded that at the time "probably not less than 30 per cent, varying from 15 to 20 per cent in the rural north and west up to 40 per cent in the countryside near London" of male inhabitants were literate and that "the rate in some of the larger towns of the south was as high as 60 per cent." See his

"Literacy and Education in England, 1640–1900," *Past and Present*, No. 42 (1969), pp. 99–102; and his "The Educational Revolution in England, 1560–1640," *ibid.*, No. 28 (1964), pp. 43–44. The question of how far an ability to sign one's name indicates also an ability to read remains debatable, but no better test seems to have been found for this period of history.

RED

PERHAPS I can best begin this discussion of the Red Virginian by observing that Captain John Smith described the native inhabitants of the Chesapeake area as being "of a colour browne."[1] Arthur Barlow, scouting the upper coast of Carolina for Sir Walter Raleigh in 1584, thought the Indians there were of a "yellowish" complexion, and John White's justly famous paintings of the Carolina natives give them a distinctly yellowish brown coloring.[2] William Strachey, who came to Virginia in 1610 as the colony's secretary, also described the Indians as "generally of a Coulour browne," but on second thought he substituted in his *Historie of Travell into Virginia Britania* the word tawny, and finally he declared that the nearest he could come to describing the general complexion of the Indian was to liken it to the color of "a sodden Quince." He explained, citing Smith, that the child at birth was an "indifferent white," and that the tawny effect was achieved by the persistent application from infancy of natural dyes mixed with walnut oil and bear's grease. He commented also upon the decorative painting of the body by the adult Indians, men and women, and upon their special fondness of a red dye taken from the Virginia pokeberry for the painting of shoulders and the head.[3] But that practice did not make the Indian a red man in Strachey's view, nor did it apparently in the view of any other Englishman who came to the colony during the period of our immediate concern. I have seen no description of the Indian in seventeenth-century Virginia that differs significantly from those already mentioned. In 1705 Robert Beverley would write in a famous account of the colony's natives: "Their Colour, when they are grown up, is a Chestnut brown and tawny; but much clearer in their Infancy.[4]

The subject of the Indian's color was one of very great interest to Europeans at the time of Virginia's first settlement and for many years thereafter. Their interest was all the greater because a long favored belief that the African's blackness was attributable to the effect of the tropical sun had been called into question by the discovery that Indians living also in the tropical zone had a different color. No single view prevailed, but certainly one underlying consideration affecting the European's approach to the problem was a need to find some explanation that fitted with the Biblical concept of creation and the belief that all mankind had a common origin. For the black African there was a simple solution in the curse of Ham, but the distinctive coloring of the Indian presented a question comparable in its difficulty to that of explaining his very presence in America.[5] Again, no single view prevailed, but there was a strong persuasion toward acceptance of the conclusion that somehow since Biblical times the Indian had come to America by way of Asia, a conclusion which conforms well enough with opinions held for quite different reasons by modern scholars as to the probability that the North American Indian originally was an immigrant from Asia.[6] As with the question of the Indian's origins, so it was that on the question of his color the view best suited to the European's preconceptions was one holding that the native American was born white and that the distinctive complexion of his skin was artificially achieved.

The point can hardly be made without a further comment upon the extent to which our knowledge of Virginia's original inhabitants depends upon the picture handed down to us by the European settler or his predecessors in the exploration of the general area. There is no time for consideration of other ways in which the picture may have been distorted by the European's preconceptions, but the question must always be kept in mind.

It is difficult to determine just when the Indian became the Redman. Evidently, it was at some time after the term *Redskin* had come into usage, and the earliest example of that usage given in the two great dictionaries of our language that have been compiled on historical principles falls in 1699, and in New England.[7] Because the Indian may have become a Redman at about the time of his elevation by Europeans to the status of a noble savage, one can wonder if some symbolical association with the color red had its influence, and this would seem to be quite possible.[8] But there can be little doubt that the usage is attributable originally to the predominance of red, as the colonist saw it, in the "warpaint" the Indian put on before taking to the "warpath." It thus serves, or it should, to remind us of the tragic failure of the two peoples to find a way of living peaceably together.

The story of the Indian in seventeenth-century Virginia is above all the story of a challenge to the white man's intrusion that is remarkable for the promptness with which it was made in the so-called massacre of 1622, for its renewal twenty-two years later in an attack which possibly cost the English more lives than had the earlier assault, and for the completeness of the defeat that had been inflicted upon the natives by mid-century. Elsewhere there were Indian wars which broke the peace of colonial communities at a comparably early time in their history. One thinks of the Pequot War in New England and Governor Kieft's War in New Netherland, but in neither of these instances can it be said that the war represented a concerted attempt by the Indians immediately affected by the presence of a white settlement to destroy that settlement. In the one instance Governor Kieft himself can be viewed as the aggressor, though not without some provocation from his foes, and in New England the Pequots were almost as much intruders as were the Puritan settlers, who seem generally to have fought the war with the friendly regard of other Indians in the area.[9] Nor can it be said that in either instance the victory won by the Europeans had quite so decisive an effect upon the colonists' subsequent relations with Indians as did the victory sealed by the peace of 1646 in Virginia.

The difference is explained, first of all, by the simple but often overlooked fact that the Virginia colony had been planted in the midst of one of the more powerful Indian communities situated along the eastern seaboard of North America. Not until the settlement of South Carolina in 1670 did an English colony find itself located in an area where the natives in their political development were comparably advanced, and even then the more powerful of the southeastern nations were a considerable distance away from Charles Town. In Maryland, the potent Susquehannahs, living along the river that still bears their name, were more or less comfortably removed from Lord Baltimore's original settlement just off the Potomac, and the problem of Indian policy had a relatively easy solution in the alliance with the Susquehannahs that held from mid-century to their dispersal by the Senecas on the eve of Bacon's Rebellion. The Dutch at New Amsterdam were surrounded by Indians, but these were divided by many jealousies, and the Dutch outpost of trade and settlement that became Albany stood outside the lands occupied by the powerful Iroquois, who held the area reaching westward from the juncture of the Mohawk River with the Hudson. In the immediate environs of the newly established Boston, war and epidemic disease had almost destroyed the Indians. The Wampanoags, remembered chiefly for the friendship they showed the Pilgrim Fathers and for their chief King Philip, who after half a century mounted a truly serious challenge to the presence of the Puritans in New England, also had been weakened by the great plague which struck the Massachusetts Bay area some four years before the Pilgrims landed. The more powerful of the Indians in New England at the beginning of Puritan settlement were the Abnaki in Maine, the Pequots in the Connecticut Valley, and the Narragansetts living west of the bay which took its name from them.[10] For the purpose of emphasizing a significant contrast, it may not be too much to suggest that the situation of Jamestown in 1607 was somewhat comparable to what might be imagined had the Dutch settled first on the Mohawk River, some distance along the way between Albany and Buffalo.

The Virginia colonists did not find it easy to describe the government of their Indian neighbors. Even so, Captain Smith, in his attempt to translate what he had observed of it into familiar European terms, seems to have done rather well, better perhaps than did Thomas Jefferson, who has been credited with being the first to describe the union over which Powhatan presided as a "Confederacy."[11] Smith said in 1612: "Although the countrie people be very barbarous, yet haue they amongst them such gouernement, as that their Magistrats for good commanding, and their people for du subiection, and obeying, excell many places that would be counted very civill. The forme of their Common wealth is a monarchicall gouernement, one as Emperour ruleth ouer many kings or governours."[12] Powhatan, Smith's "Emperour," apparently had inherited the rule of six tribes, if I may use the familiar though not altogether exact designation, and by force or the threat of force had brought the number of tribes under his sway to something like thirty.[13] His own residence seems to have been situated on the York River above Gloucester Point, at no great distance across the peninsula from the newly built fort at Jamestown. As with other such governments known to history, his power at any given time probably varied in proportion to the distance from his person.

Geographically, Powhatan's claim to jurisdiction covered most of tidewater Virginia. From the south side of the James it extended northward to the Potomac, and included two tribes of the lower Eastern Shore. He and his people belonged to the Algonkian-speaking family which occupied the coastal areas from upper Carolina to New England and well beyond. It seems to be agreed that their presence in Virginia and Carolina represents a relatively recent southward push from the main area of Algonkian occupation. Modern estimates of the total population under Powhatan's rule have ranged between eight and nine thousand. Captain Smith, whose reports serve as the main base for these estimates, declared that there were 5,000 Indians living within sixty miles of Jamestown, including possibly 1,500 warriors. Considered by itself the number is not too impressive, but it becomes much more so when one is reminded that an authoritative estimate indicates that the five Iroquois nations never could have mustered more than 2,500 warriors, or that the Virginia colony had its beginning with just over 100 men and boys.[14] However approximate may have been Smith's figures, the advantage in terms of manpower obviously belonged to Powhatan.

Why then did he not strike at once? Why, indeed, after more than seven years of an uneasy relationship between the two peoples, a relationship marked more than once by open expressions of mutual suspicion and hostility, did he make peace with the English, a peace still holding at the time of his death in 1618? The question becomes the more insistent if one accepts the suggestion that through a variety of contacts, including possibly a Spanish mission in the Chesapeake area, and almost certainly through some knowledge of the Indian's experience with Raleigh's settlers at Roanoke Island, Powhatan and his people had learned to hate the white man before the Jamestown colonists arrived.[15]

First mention perhaps belongs to the relative weakness of the English. Certainly, it cannot be assumed that the quarrelsome band of men who landed at Jamestown late in the spring of 1607 was necessarily viewed by Powhatan as a serious menace. Nor can it be said that the rate at which the Virginia colony thereafter grew was such as to give him an unmistakable warning of what lay ahead. Nine years after the first settlement, and only two years before Powhatan's death, the colony numbered no more than three hundred and fifty men, women, and children. Moreover, the intervening years had been for the English a time of great misfortune, in which more than once the simple misery of hunger had been relieved only through a trade for food with the Indians.

Powhatan may have been impressed by the European gun, as the Virginia adventurers had intended all Indians to be when instructing the first settlers never to fire their weapons in the presence of the Indian without depending upon their most expert marksmen.[16] The instruction could have been partly a precaution against the inaccuracy of the seventeenth-century musket, which some have considered to be in that regard inferior to the bow and arrow, but its firing nevertheless had a frightening effect upon the natives, and everywhere in colonial America they came to covet it and in time to possess it.[17] The palisaded fort at Jamestown, though built with a view primarily to defense against a European foe, afforded its own special protection, but it probably could not have withstood a native attack in full force, especially when its defenders were weakened by the internal strife and demoralization which frequently beset them. One has to be impressed by the relative freedom with which the English moved in small units about their several tasks.

It has been suggested that Powhatan actually may have viewed the arrival of the English at Jamestown as a development of potential advantage to him.[18] Much of his extensive empire had been recently acquired, and some of it by methods hardly to be described as gentle. He ruled as a despot, and faced the risk that disgruntled subordinates might seek to use the English against him. There was a chance, moreover, that the colonists might make common cause with

enemies of his who lived west of the fall line, an area in
which the English, hopeful of finding a passage leading to
the Orient, promptly showed a special interest. Any such
apprehension would have been by no means groundless.
Although the Virginia adventurers at first had favored a
policy of alliance with neighboring Indians against their
more distantly situated foes, they substituted the advice to
Sir Thomas Gates in 1609 that Powhatan's tribes, each and
all of them, be made tributary dependencies, and that friendship be cultivated with his enemies, the chief of whom were
specifically named.[19]

There is some reason for believing that at about the same
time Powhatan also decided upon a new policy. This apparently is when he moved his principal residence to the
upper part of the Virginia Peninsula, thereby putting a
greater distance between himself and Jamestown. It is difficult to interpret his stance theretofore in terms other than
one of watchful waiting. In the story that has come down to
us two incidents stand out. The one records Powhatan's refusal to kneel for acceptance of a copper crown brought from
England by Christopher Newport for his coronation, whether
through ignorance of what was expected or a shrewd awareness of what was implied.[20] The other is the saving of Captain Smith's life by Pocahontas. While there may remain
some doubt that the incident actually occurred, Philip Barbour recently has offered a very interesting suggestion that
the scene made so familiar to all of us through many re-
countings was ceremonial, a token of Smith's adoption into
the tribe borrowed perhaps from the puberty rites followed
in the young male's induction into full standing as a member
of the tribe, but with the emperor's daughter in this instance
assigned the starring role. Whatever may be the fact, after
1609 the Indian's resistance became more open and deadly,
and from the surviving record it becomes increasingly difficult to determine just where Powhatan was, a fact suggesting a deliberate attempt to keep the knowledge from the

English.[21] It may be well to remember that the Indian method of warfare depended more heavily upon the tactics of mobility and attrition than upon the direct assault in full force that is intended to bring a prompt and decisive victory. In other words, the North American native was willing to outwait his enemies, meanwhile punishing them whenever and wherever he could and denying to them an opportunity to retaliate. It was a stratagem the English quickly associated with stealth and other unflattering terms.

The peace that came in 1614 is difficult to interpret. No document has survived purporting to state the terms of any formal agreement that may have been reached. Secretary Ralph Hamor's *True Discourse* remains the chief source of our information regarding the peace and this leaves the distinct impression that it depended upon nothing more than the following sequence of developments: the abduction of Pocahontas by Samuel Argall in 1613; a subsequent show of force by the English and a threat to use more force; the marriage with Powhatan's consent of Pocahontas to John Rolfe; and a final mission by Hamor himself, bearing gifts and a proposal for the marriage of another of the chieftain's daughters to Sir Thomas Dale, which ended with a refusal of the marriage offer and a message from Powhatan to Dale that "hee need not distrust any iniurie from me or my people; . . . for I am now old, and would gladly end my daies in peace."[22] And so it may have been, for Hamor goes into specific detail on the conditions of a peace subsequently negotiated with the Chickahominy Indians, not the most loyal of Powhatan's people and now apparently fearful of isolation in a new and dangerous political situation.[23] Thus we are left with some right to continue believing in a peace sealed, in the best European manner, by the favorite romantic union of early American history.

It is difficult to believe, however, that Powhatan allowed sentimental considerations to influence his decision unduly, if indeed he allowed them any influence at all. He had a way of coming up with a favorite daughter whenever it was convenient, as when he advised Hamor that the young lady proposed for marriage to Dale was of all his many children the one who delighted him most. He was getting old, perhaps then past sixty, but there is no indication that he had lost any of the subtle understanding so frequently credited to him by the English with whom he dealt. The exchanges with Hamor remind one very much of those recorded by Smith, who obviously, even when some discount is made for the captain's desire to enhance his own reputation, had great respect for Powhatan. The war had been costly to the Indians as well as to the English. The suit for peace by the powerful Chickahominys argues both that Powhatan had a need to consolidate his own authority and that he was still feared by his fellows. Perhaps he was influenced by the declining strength of the English colony, or perhaps he had made a realistic assessment of the persistence with which the London adventurers continued to supply their colony despite repeated misfortunes, and so had given up whatever hope he originally may have had that the colonists, like Raleigh's people, sooner or later would abandon their efforts and go away. Perhaps, above all, he wanted to renew a trade with the English.

His people had a relatively sophisticated economy. It depended basically upon agriculture—a point of very great importance for an understanding of much that was to follow, not to mention much of the Southern diet down to the present day—and the foodstuff they grew was richly supplemented by hunting and fishing. The three crops of Indian corn they cultivated each year was for the European one of the marvels of the New World.[24] Any suggestion that they were an improvident people, living from hand to mouth and lacking provision for the storage of a surplus production, is easily dismissed simply by recalling the number of occasions on which the colonists, both at Roanoke Island and Jamestown, were fed by corn secured from the Indians at different seasons of the year. Their hunting for the wild turkey, the beaver, and especially the deer, which supplied in addition to its meat important items for clothing and even for tools, could be a highly organized communal enterprise pursued with such perseverance that the English found early occasions to comment upon the scarcity of deer in the lower part of the Virginia Peninsula.[25] As for their fishing, they ate a variety of seafood as great as the methods they employed in catching it by use of the weir, the net, the fishhook, the spear, and the arrow. Their "canoes," not the birch-covered canoe of the more northerly situated Indians but a vessel shaped out of a single log, might carry, according to Smith, as many as 40 men apiece.[26] The implements they had contrived showed much sophistication, some of them being quite similar in form and function to the more familiar tools of the European, but they were not made of metal. The one metal they seem to have had was copper, which was highly prized but apparently used only for ornamental purposes.[27]

In our textbooks, discussions of the early trade with the Indians tend to feature an exchange of beads and other "trifles" for the corn which at times quite literally kept the colonists from starving. It is true enough that the Indian was fond of ornamentation, and that he frequently took beads for his corn, but he also had a sharp eye for things of more substance the Englishman possessed. Captain Smith complained that, before he took over as president of the colony in 1608, "of 2. or 300 hatchets, chissels, mattocks, and pickaxes scarce 20 could be found" within six or seven weeks after the departure for England of the ship bringing the supply, and he attributed this largely to pilfering for the purposes of a private trade with the Indians. In 1612, after describing the native tomahawk and its use as a weapon, he added: "This they were wont to vse also for hatchets, but now by trucking they haue plenty of the same forme of yron." William Strachey, speaking of this same weapon and tool, declared that "now by trucking with vs, they haue thowsandes of our Iron hatchetts such as they be."[28] This last phrase is rather intriguing. I have no evidence that the English at this early date were making a cheap hatchet for the Indian market, as much later they would a cheap gun, but it does sound as though not all of the hatchets shipped to Virginia were of the best grade.

It probably is too early in our story to begin talking of the Indian's rapid transition from the Stone Age to the Iron Age, and of the potentially destructive effect of this transition upon his own culture. No doubt the emphasis here belongs to the native's quick awareness of the advantages he might enjoy by drawing upon the superior technology of the European. When Ralph Hamor went on his mission to Powhatan he carried as presents from Dale two large pieces of copper, five strings of white and blue beads, five wooden combs, ten fishhooks, a pair of knives, and the promise of a "great grinding stone." On his return to Jamestown he brought what amounted to an order from Powhatan, with the promise of payment in skins, for ten pieces of copper, "a shauing knife, an iron frow to cleaue bordes," a grindstone not larger than could be carried by four or five men, two bone combs (Powhatan advised that his own men could make wooden combs), one hundred fishhooks, or if it could be spared, "rather a fishing saine," a cat, and a dog.[29]

After this, little more is heard of Powhatan except as the father of the more famous of his most cherished daughters, who in 1616 moved to center-stage in a well managed visit to England. Samuel Argall reported in 1617 that he had gone to the Potomac, leaving the government to Opechancanough and "his other brother," and early in 1618 that he "goes from place to place visiting his Country taking his pleasure in good friendship with us." In the following June, John Rolfe reported that Powhatan had died in the preceding April, that his brother Opitchapan had succeeded him,

and that both "hee and Opechancanough haue confirmed
our former league."[30]

Opechancanough, who quickly became Powhatan's real
successor, remains a very shadowy figure, despite the fact
that the leaders of the colony from Captain Smith forward
repeatedly had dealt with him as a half-brother in whom
the emperor placed a special confidence, and as head of the
Pamunkeys, one of the original tribes owing allegiance to
Powhatan and perhaps the most powerful. There may or
may not be an element of truth in the tradition, apparently
first recorded by Robert Beverley, that he actually was an
outsider who had come "a great Way from the South-West."
More to the point is Beverley's description of him as "a Man
of large stature, noble Presence, and extraordinary Parts."[31]
Of this last we can be certain, for it was he who planned and
staged both of the great massacres.

In using the term massacre, I am reminded that some one
has observed that when the Indian and the white man fought
in this country, the fight became a battle when the white man
won, a massacre when the Indian prevailed. This doubtless is
true enough, but the colonists who escaped the attack that
came on Good Friday morning of 1622 were fully justified in
describing it as a massacre. Although the normal practice of
the Indians was to spare women and children to become a
prize of war held for enslavement, adoption, or marriage, and
although on this occasion there is evidence that perhaps as
many as twenty persons survived as prisoners, in most places
men, women, and children were slaughtered indiscrim-
inately.[32] Opechancanough unmistakably intended to destroy the colony through a single coordinated assault upon
plantations stretched out along both banks of the James in a
dangerously dispersed pattern of settlement that the English
had allowed to develop over the course of the preceding four
years. It cannot be said that the warriors he deployed that
morning represented the full force of the so-called Powhatan

Indians, for the Potomacs and evidently those living on the
Eastern Shore did not participate in the attack.[33] Nor can it
be said that the surprise achieved was quite so complete as
tradition would have us believe, but it is hardly the less remarkable. The casualties inflicted, though falling far short of
what Opechancanough undoubtedly had hoped for, could
have been higher than the officially admitted figure of 347
dead. The serious dislocations resulting from the massacre,
together with an epidemic which followed it, brought the
colony all too close to the destruction Opechancanough had
intended to inflict upon it.[34]

The colonists were quick to find an explanation couched
in the simple terms of barbarism, savagery, and treachery.
Their bitterness was all the greater because Opechancanough's repeated assurances of his peaceable intentions had
coincided with moves by the English adventurers to provide the most substantial evidence yet given of their good
will toward the Indian. For all the skepticism with which the
modern student has read the record, the adventurers from
the first had assigned a high place among their objectives to
the Indian's conversion to the Christian faith, and at the
time of the massacre they were engaged in launching a major
missionary undertaking in the Indian school and college that
was to depend for support very largely upon funds raised as
a result of the earlier visit by Pocahontas to England.[35] However misguided may have been this effort, there can be no
question as to the sincerity of the convictions upon which
the project rested, or the justification for their own conduct
the colonists found in it. But the question of good will or ill
will is really beside the main point to be made here. Although
the English adventurers had given much thought to the problem of getting along with the Indian, they had no solution
for an accommodation of the two peoples that did not depend
upon an assumption that the Indian in time would adapt to
a European pattern of life. What the massacre signalled
above all was the Indian's refusal to adapt.

That refusal is not difficult to understand. He had his own culture, and the normal loyalty of any people to their own heritage.[36] Whatever one may think of the despotism of Powhatan and Opechancanough, the political system over which they presided offered protection for its members against their foes, of whom all Indians seem to have had many. The sophistication of the economy already has been mentioned, and did time permit, additional comment could be made on the sophistication of the Powhatans in the development of arts and crafts, including their pottery, basketry, and the pipes in which they smoked the tobacco they grew, or the musical instrument made from a reed that John Smith compared with the recorder, then very popular in England.[37] The division of labor between the sexes often has been misunderstood by the modern American, perhaps because he equates hunting and fishing too much with sport. One reads European discussions of the Indian's religion with less assurance than is felt in reading descriptions of other aspects of native life, no doubt because the questions asked by the European of the Indian were so deeply rooted in the Christian tradition. Suffice it to say that the Indian's religion was a form of pantheism, and that the frequently miserable estate of the colonists at Jamestown must have persuaded more than one Indian that his own gods were as powerful as any the English had to offer. Ralph Lane has recorded for us the open contempt shown toward the English near the end of Raleigh's first colony by the local Indians, who began "flatly to say, that our Lord God was not God, since hee suffered vs to sustaine much hunger, and also to be killed of the Renapoaks," this last a generic name Lane understood to comprehend the whole of the mainland Indians.[38]

The English, whose attitude toward the native culture was at its best patronizing, had been quick to see in the Indian priest a dangerous foe. As early as 1609 Gates was authorized, in a section of his instructions dealing with a plan for bring-

ing up Indian children in English households, to imprison
all of the priests if he saw fit, and he was further advised not
to hesitate to deal even "more sharply with . . . these mur-
therers of Soules."[39] William Strachey regarded the priests
as the chief instigators of attacks upon the colonists. He
depicted them, and probably with good reason, as warning
their chieftains of the offence that would be given the Indian
gods if "a Nation despising the auncyent Religion of their
forfathers" be permitted "to inhabite among them." By way
of illustrating the influence of the priests, he tells of a
prophesy made to Powhatan that a nation would "arise"
from Chesapeake Bay to destroy his empire, and to this
prophesy Strachey attributes the destruction of the Chesapeake Indians, who formerly had lived just below the bay
that still bears their name but were described at the time of
Strachey's writing as being extinct. Especially interesting is
the fact that his account of the destruction of the Chesapeakes
is followed immediately in the text by a report, received
from "some of the Inhabitants," that still another prophesy
had been made, this one foretelling "that twice" Powhatan's
people might overthrow "such Straungers as should envade
their Territoryes, or laboure to settell a plantation amongest
them, but the third tyme they themselves should fall into
their Subiection and vnder their Conquest."[40]

It seems obvious enough that Powhatan was not persuaded
to act on this or any other such prophesy. Nor can it be said
that a decade later Opechancanough did so. But it can be
said that if the latter's policy through four years, in which
he more than once renewed the peace, was to bide his time,
there was warning enough for him in the swelling migration
from England after 1618—a migration fixed by the Virginia
Company at more than three thousand, five hundred persons—that time was running out.[41] The number of Indians
converted to the Christian faith before 1622 was hardly large
enough to disturb any save the most apprehensive of the
native priests, but perhaps in situations like this it is not

the number of conversions, or defections, that really counts.
In any case, it seems worthy of note that it was a converted
Indian who gave the warning on the morning of the massacre
that was credited with saving Jamestown.[42]

The embittered colonists lacked the strength and the aid
from England to carry out the advice of the Virginia Company that their enemies no longer be allowed to live as "a
people vppon the face of the Earth."[43] But the colony did
manage, in the pursuit of a policy once described as one of
"perpetual enmity," to field year after year forces whose task
was systematically to cut the Indian's corn in the field, burn
his villages, destroy his fishing weirs, and subject him to
every other possible harassment. Through these tactics the
colonists kept the area of settlement reasonably clear of Indians, and having established early in the 1630s a frontier
outpost in the promoted settlement at Chiskiack on the York
River, the government finally allowed the kind of peace that
is broken only by individual incidents to return.[44]

After another decade had passed, Opechancanough struck
again. This time the venture was foolhardy in the extreme.
Perhaps his age was to blame. There is no way of telling just
what it was, but he was considerably older than the colony
itself, and Beverley has reported that he was now virtually
blind and so infirm that he had to be carried to the field of
battle. His attack, which apparently came in April 1644,
brought death to perhaps as many as five hundred colonists,
but the casualties seem to have been sustained mainly by the
outlying settlements of a colony then numbering probably
more than eight thousand persons. The resulting war dragged
on for two years, and it was probably in the second of these
years that Opechancanough himself was captured and carried
to Jamestown, where, according to tradition, he died after
being shot in the back by a soldier set to guard him.[45] The
progress of the war is recorded for us by the assembly's provision in 1645 for the building of three blockhouses intended
to protect the colonists against further attacks by the In-

dians, one at the falls of the James, another at Pamunkey on
the Mattaponi, and a third overlooking the Chickahominy;
in the following year provision was made for a fourth fort
at the falls of the Appomattox.[46] By March 1646 it was
concluded by the General Assembly that there was little
point in continuing the war. The Indians were described as
"driven from their townes and habitations, lurking up &
downe the woods in small numbers," and it was agreed that
it would be almost impossible to impose any "further revenge
upon" them.[47] The time had come for a peace.

The distinguishing feature of the peace of 1646, recorded
for us in the form of a statute adopted by a general assembly
meeting in October of that year, was a provision making
the defeated Indians tributary to the government of the
colony. It was not a new idea. Such a proposal had been made
as early as 1609, but with a significant difference. The
thought then had been to destroy Powhatan's authority by
making the tribes individually dependent upon the English,
who would rely for discipline of the tributary Indians upon
an alliance with their enemies. Now the decision was to preserve at least some semblance of the old union as a device
for giving effect to the new tributary status and to an alliance
with the tributary Indians against their foes. Hence the
distinction between "neighboring" or "friendly" Indians
and "foreign" Indians that runs through virtually all discussion of the Indian problem for the remainder of the
century.[48]

By the terms of the treaty Necotowance, who was described simply as "king of the Indians" and who presumably
was successor to Opechancanough, acknowledged that he held
his lands of the king of England by payment of "twenty
beaver skins att the goeing away of Geese yearely."[49] It was
further provided that no Indian, without special permission
and upon the pain of death, could enter any part of the
peninsula lying below the falls of the York and James Rivers,
and that on the south side of the latter stream no Indian

could come closer to the English plantations than a line running straight from the head of Blackwater River to "old Monakin town," which lay above the falls of the James. There was nothing new in this attempt to exclude the Indian from the main areas of settlement; it merely extended the limits of the area from which he was to be excluded. There was, however, a new element of policy, one pointing unmistakably toward the Indian reservations of later date, in the attempt to establish an exclusive right of the Indians to the land lying across the York River, except for the governor's option, after giving notice, to open the lower reaches of the river to settlement by the English. This provision would appear to have been intended as a guarantee principally for the Pamunkeys, Opechancanough's tribe, but the phrasing is so vague that it is impossible to know how far north the guarantee may have been intended to reach, as it also is impossible to say how far in any direction the authority of the new "king of the Indians" actually extended. But one point is certain: whatever authority he held, or might hold thereafter, belonged to him by the sufferance of the English colony. Nowhere is the completeness of the Indian's defeat more clearly recorded than in the treaty's provision that thereafter the governor of Virginia would determine, by confirmation or appointment, the succession to the office of "king of the Indians."

There seems to be no information available for an answer to the question of how long Necotowance may have remained in office, but apparently it was not long. A promotional pamphlet published in London in 1649 reports his visit in the preceding year to Sir William Berkeley, "with five more petty kings attending him," to make payment of the twenty beaver skins and to protest that "the sun and moon should first lose their glorious lights . . . before he, or his people should evermore hereafter wrong the English in any kind," but after that, so far as I have found, he simply drops out of history.[50] I have seen no firm evidence that he even had a successor as "king of the Indians."[51] Certainly the surviving records of the colony indicate that its government quickly came to deal with the several tribes individually rather than collectively.

How complete a defeat had been inflicted upon the Indians is also demonstrated by their failure to put up any serious resistance to the extraordinary expansion of the area of English settlement which followed soon after the peace of 1646, a peace it may be well to remember that was made at a time when the migration from England was in marked decline. The land across the lower York was opened for settlement as early as 1648, the same year in which Northumberland County on the lower Potomac was formed. As the migration from England gained momentum, the intervening region, drained chiefly by the Rappahannock, was occupied. Before 1660 the settlers were pushing up both of these rivers toward the fall line, while below the James the settled area drew closer to the lands of the Iroquoian Nottaways and Meherrins, who apparently had never paid tribute to Powhatan or Opechancanough. Trouble might develop here and there, as when early in the 1650s an alarm was raised about the intentions of the Rappahannock Indians, and the local militia was authorized to take such action as might be necessary. There is no indication, however, that whatever action may have been undertaken involved a conflict of serious proportions. By the 1660s it had become a virtually established principle of the colony's policy that each community could and would take care of its own Indian troubles.[52]

It is not intended to suggest that the government at Jamestown became indifferent to a problem that was much more likely to involve individual acts of violence, both by the settler and by the Indian, than a return to open warfare. The provincial authorities normally confined their own activity to two main areas. First, they struggled—and I think it has to be said honestly—to reduce the risk of trouble by providing simple justice for the tributary Indians under circumstances in which some intermingling of the two peoples seemed to be inescapable.[53] Claiming special and repeated attention was the difficult question of how to protect the Indian's right to a fair share of the land. Secondly, they sought to tighten the government's disciplinary control over the several tribes, and most notably by a statute of 1665 which deprived the tributary Indians of even so much as the semblance of a right to choose their own leaders. Their choice since 1646 had been subject to the governor's confirmation, but now he was authorized to select as commanders of the "respective towns" such persons as he had cause to place confidence in. The penalty for disobedience to, or the murder of, a chieftain so appointed was the loss of status as friendly Indians.[54]

This was a penalty only the more irresponsible of Indians could then have thought it safe to ignore. Not only were the natives divided politically and confronted by an immigration of such overwhelming proportions as to reemphasize each year their relative weakness, but over the preceding decades they themselves had suffered an extraordinary actual loss in numbers. A continuing plague of wolves, which more than once before had led the assembly to seek aid from the Indians, brought in October 1669 an act assigning to each of the tributary tribes an annual quota of wolf heads, and because the quotas were assessed according to the number of hunters in each of the tribes, the act provides an unusually valuable indication of their strength individually and collectively.[55] There were now no more than nineteen tributary tribes, not counting those on the Eastern Shore and including several which had not been among the some thirty tribes Powhatan once controlled. Those tribes which can be identified as former members of his "confederacy" had in 1669 a total of 528 warriors, a figure to be compared with the some 2,400 credited to Powhatan's command by Captain John Smith. On the basis of the data provided by the act of 1669, it has been estimated that the total population of the Powhatan Indians had fallen since 1607 from eight or nine thousand to perhaps no more than two thousand.[56]

Hardly less significant than this marked decline in strength is the inclusion among the tributary tribes in 1669 of Indians who had not been a part of Powhatan's empire. Two towns of the Nottoway Indians, with a combined muster of ninety warriors, outranked in size all other tributary groups. The fifty warriors listed for the Meherrins gave them place also among the more powerful of the friendly tribes. Much less impressive were the thirty men representing what must have been a very small remnant of the Monacans, who on the upper James had been regarded by Powhatan as one of his more dangerous foes.[57] Just when these outlying tribes had come to terms with the English seems uncertain, but their inclusion in the list serves to remind us that at some time before 1669 an entirely new chapter in the history of the colony's Indian relations had been opened.

How early that chapter may have had its beginning is suggested by the military action the colony took in 1656 against a body of strange Indians, known to the colonists as the Richeharians, who had taken up a position in the neighborhood of modern Richmond. Who they were remains an unsettled question. It has been suggested that they may have been Cherokees who had come from the southwest for no other purpose than a trade with the English. Another view is that they probably were some remnant of the Manahoacs, who in Powhatan's day had occupied the upper reaches of the Rappahannock, posing an even more serious challenge to his empire than did their allies the Monacans, and who now had been driven down by the hostile action of other Indians, possibly the Susquehannahs. Whatever may be the fact, they were "foreign" Indians and the English settlers with their native allies made the intruder's expulsion a common cause. The forces sent against them included one hundred militiamen from the upper James River counties and one hundred Pamunkey warriors. The resulting fight has gone down in history as a defeat for the allied forces, no doubt in part because the king of the Pamunkeys was killed together with many of his warriors.[58] Perhaps it was a defeat, but it hardly could have been more than a momentary reversal.

Much more pertinent to the purposes of the present discussion is the evidence which argues that before 1669 the western frontiers of the Virginia colony, running then roughly with the fall line, had been cleared of more or less permanent Indian residents who were capable of posing a serious challenge to the colony, or even to its further expansion in that direction. The Manahoacs had disappeared, possibly through defeats suffered at the hands of Powhatan or Opechancanough, who through eight years of peace with the English had opportunities to settle a score with their native enemies, or perhaps later through invasions from the north by the Susquehannahs or other warlike Indians, or conceivably through some combination of all these possibilities. To the previously mentioned thirty bowmen representing a remnant of the once feared Monacans must be added still another remnant, the Saponi, who lived farther west, some of them in the neighborhood, I believe, of Charlottesville. In 1669 the Saponi presumably were still independent, but they came to terms with the English in the peace of 1677 that followed Bacon's Rebellion.[59]

As early as 1662 the colony's records make it evident that the critical aspect of the Indian problem was becoming the intrusions of Indians whom the government might simply describe as the Northern Indians, or with some possible confusion of identities as Susquehannahs, Doegs, or Marylanders.[60] A part of the trouble was blamed also on the king of the Potomacs, one of the earlier Powhatan tribes which finds no place among the tributary Indians in 1669. The story is a difficult one for the modern student to reconstruct, but there can be little doubt as to the ultimate source of the

trouble.[61] The North American Indians were divided by
many jealousies, some of them ancient, and more to the
point, some of them sharpened by the presence of the European—none more than those involving the Iroquois Confed-
eration of New York. Strategically situated for gaining an
advantage from the presence of virtually all the European
nations active in North America, saving only Spain, they
fought during the middle years of the seventeenth century a
succession of wars that brought destruction or dispersal first
to the Hurons in Canada, next to the Eries in western New
York and Pennsylvania, and finally to the Susquehannahs.[62]
It has been suggested that the Susquehannahs enjoyed the
greatest freedom for adventures of their own while the
Iroquois were concentrating on the destruction of the Eries,
a task finally completed by 1656, and that the subsequent and
protracted struggle between the Iroquois and the Susquehannahs afforded comparable opportunities for adventure
by other northern Indians.[63] We can be certain only that it
was the defeat and dispersal of the Susquehannahs which
brought about the crisis on Virginia's northwestern frontier
leading finally to Bacon's Rebellion.

How far the friendly Indians of Virginia may have gotten
out of hand in the early months of 1676 probably must remain a question on which opinions will differ. The record
itself is difficult to interpret, if only because the colonists,
or most of them at least, were disinclined to draw any distinction between one Indian and another and so blamed them
all. It is my own opinion that the hysterical fear which seized
the colonists after the initial attack in January caused them
to exaggerate the number of hostile acts by Indians, friendly
or other. Be that as it may, it is a matter of record that the
Pamunkeys, who among the tributary tribes became the
chief target of the settlers' wrath, were subsequently exon-
erated by the investigation of royal commissioners who included Francis Moryson, an experienced leader in the colony
for many years past.[64] The one point on which full agree-

ment can be had is that the tributary Indians then had
passed through another bitter and undoubtedly debilitating
experience.

Once more, in the spring of 1677, they acknowledged their
allegiance to the king of England and received renewed guar-
antees of their own rights. But the relationship of the two
peoples continued to be poisoned by doubts as to the Indian's
fidelity which the colonists, and their government, had carried
over from the time of Bacon's Rebellion. The fear fed by
these doubts might have quickly subsided, except for the
fact that the colony continued to experience trouble with
Indians along its frontiers, and especially in the northwest.
Historians have become accustomed to interpret such difficulties as almost invariably the result of a clash between the
advancing settler and the Indian confronted by still another
demand that he yield up more of his land, but in this instance, at least, a quite different reading seems to be required.
Not only had the area lying immediately west of the colony's
frontier been cleared generally of the Indians formerly in-
habiting there, but this was especially true of the upper
extension of the frontier, where most of the trouble seems
to have occurred. Moreover, Lord Culpeper's proprietary
grant to the region recently had called into serious question
the policies that henceforth would govern its development,
and there seems little reason for assuming that the special
pressures of a rapidly expanding area of settlement could
have been in any way the critical factor.[65] A much more
convincing view is that repeatedly expressed as the view
of the colony's government, which promptly placed the chief
blame upon roving bands of Iroquois warriors, and especially the Senecas, whose name in the colony's records became
now almost interchangeable with the old designation
"Northern Indians." It was recognized that the Senecas,
following familiar warpaths south, could be as dangerous to
the tributary Indians as to the isolated settler, but this reali-
zation also was coupled with the fear that the friendly In-

dians might make common cause with the intruders.[66] Maryland was experiencing similar difficulties with the Iroquois, and as early as 1677 the two governments undertook jointly sponsored negotiations at Albany for the security of their frontiers. A treaty negotiated by Virginia at Albany in 1684 helped to ease the tension along that colony's frontiers.[67]

These negotiations were merely the earliest in which Virginia would be involved. The Iroquois sought with great persistence to extend their influence southward, across a backcountry remarkably free of Indians capable of resistance until the lands belonging to the Cherokee had been reached. But the later chapters of this story have no place here.

The space belongs instead to the marked decline in the fortunes of Virginia's tributary Indians during the last quarter of the seventeenth century. In 1697, Sir Edmund Andros, then approaching the end of his term as governor, reported to the newly established Board of Trade that the tributary Indians were capable of mustering hardly as many as three hundred and sixty-two bowmen, of whom almost one hundred were credited to nine small "nations" on the Eastern Shore, which probably had nowhere near that strength.[68] If it be remembered that the muster roll of 1669 did not include the Eastern Shore Indians, the contrast is even more marked than at first glance it appears, for where formerly there had been considerably more than 528 warriors there were now less than half that number. Perhaps an even more impressive indication of the declining strength of Virginia's Indians is found in the extraordinarily sympathetic account of them published in 1705 in Robert Beverley's *History and Present State of Virginia*. The challenge the Indians once had made to the presence of the English had become a part of history, a history that could deal generously even with Opechancanough. Although Governor Andros had reported in 1697 that "no endeavours to convert the Indians to Christianity have ever been heard of," the newly chartered College of William and Mary was destined ere long to turn its attention to the mission once promised for the projected Indian school of the 1620s. The history was coming full circle, and the English still had no solution for the Indian problem that did not depend upon the hope that the native ultimately would make the adaptation he earlier had so obviously and bitterly rejected.

Explanations that usually have been offered for the remarkable decline of Virginia's Indians to the status of a harmless curiosity understandably begin with the toll exacted by war. It probably would be a mistake, however, to think in terms primarily of combat casualties. Not only were the Indian's tactics skillfully adapted to a need to reduce casualties, but he knew when to retreat and how to take advantage of the cover generously provided by a familiar environment. Undoubtedly, the cumulative toll taken over so protracted a period of hostilities as that following the first massacre was significant, but it seems likely that the hunger, exposure, and psychological shock resulting from the tactics employed by the English were much more costly. There was also for the Indian the continuing toll resulting from the attitude of colonists who had learned to take "small account of shedding Indians' blood, though never so innocent," in the phrasing of a statute of 1656 intended to provide a remedy.[69] After the massacre of 1644, some of the Indians taken as prisoners were shipped out of the colony, presumably for sale as slaves.[70] Finally, there were those who simply fled in search of a refuge outside the area of settlement, not always finding it, and those who fell victims to intruding "foreign" Indians.[71]

It is reasonable to assume, as often it has been, that the toll taken by unfamiliar diseases brought in by the English was high, but it has to be said that in the case of Virginia's Indians very scanty evidence indeed exists to support the view. There is evidence that after 1667, when apparently the first recorded epidemic of smallpox in the colony's history occurred, the natives suffered seriously, especially on the Eastern Shore, but that is just about the sum of it.[72] Beverley

declared that they were not subject to many diseases. The
Rev. John Clayton, himself a physician, in 1687 wrote re-
spectfully of a number of their medical practices, described
the Indians as persons generally well proportioned and tall
(as had others before him), and spoke of the declining size
of the population as something of a puzzle in view of the
fact that they lived "under the English protection & have no
violence offered them." In this connection, he included an
interesting demographic comment. He reported that although some Indians had lived to a very old age, he was
unable to say that there was any remarkable difference in this
regard between the Indians and the colonists, who if they
lived "past 33 they generally live to a good age; but many
die between 30 & 33." And to this he added, speaking of the
natives: "They are undoubtedly no great breeders."[73]

Economic considerations have received much less attention than the subject deserves. A close study in this connection of the Indian trade probably would reveal much that is
helpful. The point that has to be kept in mind is how quickly the advantage in this trade passed from the neighboring
Indians to those more distantly situated from the colony,
whether for political reasons, as after the massacre of 1622,
or because of a depletion in the local supply of skins through
the over-hunting the trade itself encouraged. As is well
known, the main thrust of the Virginia traders after 1622
was toward the upper Chesapeake, with William Claiborne
in the lead, and by mid-century toward the south and south-
west with Abraham Wood and later William Byrd as leaders.
That some trade with the tributary tribes was reestablished
after 1646 is indicated by the assembly's concern in 1662 lest
the intrusions of the "Northern Indians" deprive the colony's
own Indians of the means for a trade upon which their
livelihood then depended.[74]

Certainly, in other parts of North America the Indians
who survived the intrusion of the Europeans with strength
enough to gain an advantage over other Indians, to demand

respectful attention from representatives of the European powers, and to preserve their own culture without sacrifice of dignity, however temporarily in the long run, were those who could trade with the European more or less on equal terms. Where this became impossible the Indian became dependent, a man destined to serve at best in the capacity of an interpreter or a scout, a man often despised and hated by the ordinary colonist, if not by his more enlightened leaders. I see no reason for assuming that Virginia's Indians had a different fate.

Notes

1. In his *Map of Virginia*, published at Oxford in 1612. See Edward Arber and A. G. Bradley, *Travels and Works of Captain John Smith* (Edinburgh, 1910), I, 65.

2. David B. Quinn, *The Roanoke Voyages, 1584–1590* (London, 1955) I, 102; and for White's paintings, Paul Hulton and David B. Quinn, *The American Drawings of John White, 1577–1590, with Drawings of European and Oriental Subjects* (Chapel Hill, N.C., 1964), a work containing decidedly the best reproductions of the originals.

3. Louis B. Wright and Virginia Freund, *The Historie of Travell into Virginia Britania (1612) by William Strachey, gent.* (London, 1953), pp. 70–71.

4. Beverley, *The History and Present State of Virginia* ed. Louis B. Wright (Chapel Hill, N.C., 1947), p. 159. For other such descriptions see an account of 1689 attributed to the Reverend John Clayton, in *William and Mary Quarterly*, 3d ser., XVI (1959), 230; John Lawson, *A New Voyage to Carolina* (1709) ed. Hugh T. Lefler (Chapel Hill, N.C., 1967), p. 174; Father Andrew White in 1634, in Clayton C. Hall, *Narratives of Early Maryland* (New York, 1910), pp. 42–43; and *ibid.*, p. 366 for George Alsop's description in 1666 of the Susquehannahs: "Their skins are naturally white, but altered from their original by the several dyings of Roots and Barks, that they prepare and make useful to metamorphize their hydes into a dark Cinamon brown."

5. See especially the discussion in Winthrop D. Jordan, *White over Black: American Attitudes toward the Negro, 1550–1812* (Chapel Hill, N.C., 1968), pp. 11–20, 239–52.

6. A recent study of ideas debated among Europeans is Lee E. Hud-

dleston, *Origins of the American Indians: European Concepts, 1492–1729* (Austin, Tex., 1967). For Strachey's discussion, see *Historie*, pp. 53–55; and for that of Hugh Jones, *The Present State of Virginia*, ed. Richard L. Morton (Chapel Hill, N.C., 1956), pp. 49–53, where incidentally he speaks of the Indian's "copper colour."

7. In both the OED and the Craigie dictionary of American usages, the citation is to a letter of Samuel Smith of Hadley, Mass., printed in Helen E. Smith, *Colonial Days and Ways* (New York, 1901), pp. 48–52.

8. There is a certain ambivalence in the symbolism identified with the color red. It had a traditional identification with the vendetta, and of course with blood; on the other hand, it had associations with the sun, health, and in combination with white, beauty. See Jordan, *White over Black*, pp. 8–9, 143; P. J. Heather, "Color Symbolism," *Folk Lore*, LIX (1948), 165–83; LX (1949), 316–31; and Don Cameron Allen, "Symbolic Color in the Literature of the English Renaissance," *Philological Quarterly*, XV (1936), 81–92.

9. I follow here Allen W. Trelease, *Indian Affairs in Colonial New York: The Seventeenth Century* (Ithaca, N.Y., 1960), pp. 60–84; and Alden T. Vaughan, *New England Frontier: Puritans and Indians, 1620–1675* (Boston, 1965), pp. 55–56, 134–38.

10. See Harold E. Driver, *Indians of North America* (Chicago, 1969), pp. 302–4; John R. Swanton, *The Indians of the Southeastern United States* (Washington, 1946); Raphael Semmes, *Captains and Mariners of Early Maryland* (Baltimore, 1937), pp. 504–38; Trelease, *Indian Affairs in New York*, p. 124; Vaughan, *New England Frontier*, pp. 21–22, 27–63.

11. Nancy O. Lurie, "Indian Cultural Adjustment to European Civilization," in James M. Smith, *Seventeenth-Century America: Essays in Colonial History* (Chapel Hill, N.C., 1959), p. 40.

12. Philip L. Barbour, *The Jamestown Voyages Under the First Charter, 1606–1609* (Cambridge, Eng., 1969), II, 369.

13. Authorities differ on the total number. See Lurie, "Indian Cultural Adjustment," p. 40; and Ben C. McCary, *Indians in Seventeenth-Century Virginia* (Williamsburg, Va., 1957), pp. 1–10, for a helpful listing of the tribes with their locations. Smith's account and his map remain, of course, the basic source. For one of the many reproductions of the map, see Barbour's *Jamestown Voyages*, II, 374.

14. *Ibid.*, II, 354, for Smith's figures. James Mooney, "The Aboriginal Population of America North of Mexico," *Smithsonian Miscellaneous Collections*, LXXX (1928), No. 7, p. 6, gives nine thousand, but see Maurice A. Mook, "The Aboriginal Population of Tidewater Virginia," *American Anthropologist*, XLVI (1946), 193–208. For the Iroquois, see Trelease, *Indian Affairs*, p. 16.

15. James Mooney, "The Powhatan Confederacy, Past and Present," *American Anthropologist*, IX (1907), 129–52; and Clifford M. Lewis and Albert J. Loomie, *The Spanish Jesuit Mission in Virginia, 1570–1572* (Chapel Hill, N.C., 1953).

16. Barbour, *Jamestown Voyages*, I, 52.

17. Driver, *Indians of North America*, p. 310; Carl P. Russell, *Guns on the Early Frontiers: A History of Firearms from Colonial Times through the Years of the Western Fur Trade* (Berkeley and Los Angeles, 1962).

18. Lurie, "Indian Cultural Adjustment," pp. 43–44.

19. Susan M. Kingsbury, *Records of the Virginia Company of London* (Washington, 1906–35), III, 18–21. It should be noted that these instructions indicate that the adventurers were considering a move of the colony's principal seat to a point above the falls or on the Chowan River.

20. John Smith, *Travels and Works*, I, 121–25.

21. Philip L. Barbour, *Pocahontas and Her World* (Boston, 1970), pp. 24–25 for the Pocahontas incident. His narrative of subsequent developments is unusually well informed.

22. Ralph Hamor, *A True Discourse of the Present State of Virginia* (Richmond, 1957), a facsimile reprint of the first issue of 1615, pp. 1–11, 37–42. For the quotation, see John Smith, *Travels and Works*, II, 519, where the phrasing is slightly different from that in the original.

23. Hamor, *True Discourse*, pp. 11–14.

24. See Quinn, *Roanoke Voyages*, I, 317–87, for Thomas Hariot's especially famous account of the Carolina Indians; and Barbour, *Jamestown Voyages*, II, 350–53, 357, 358–60, for passages in Smith's *Map of Virginia* that are especially pertinent; and Hulton and Quinn, *The American Drawings of John White*, for White's painting of "The Towne of Secota," which dramatically reveals the interest taken in the Indian's corn.

25. Barbour, *Jamestown Voyages*, II, 359; Bruce, *Economic History*, I, 124; Kingsbury, *Records of the Virginia Company*, III, 557.

26. Again, one of White's paintings, illustrating the technique employed in its production, is the best reference.

27. For the possible sources of supply, see Henry Lee Reynolds, "Algonkin Metal-Smiths," *American Anthropologist*, I, 341–52; Bruce, *Economic History*, I, 82–83.

28. Barbour, *Jamestown Voyages*, II, 358, 417; Strachey, *Historie of Travell*, p. 109.

29. Hamor, *True Discourse*, pp. 40, 45.

30. Kingsbury, *Records of the Virginia Company*, III, 73–74, 92; John Smith, *Travels and Works*, II, 539.

31. Beverley, *History*, p. 61.

32. For Smith's account of the Indian custom, see Barbour, *Jamestown Voyages*, II, 360–62. See also Strachey, *Historie of Travell*, pp. 104–5; Driver, *Indians of North America*, p. 324. For the prisoners in 1622, see Kingsbury, *Records of the Virginia Company*, IV, 98–99; and III, 565–71, for a list of those killed.

33. Kingsbury, *Records of the Virginia Company*, IV, 89; Susie M. Ames, *Studies of the Virginia Eastern Shore in the Seventeenth Century* (Richmond, 1940), pp. 5–6.

34. The fullest of recent accounts of the massacre and its consequences

is found in Richard Beale Davis, *George Sandys: Poet-Adventurer* (London and New York, 1955), pp. 126–62.

35. See Perry Miller, "The Religious Impulse in the Founding of Virginia," *William and Mary Quarterly*, 3d ser., V (1948), 492–522, and VI (1949), 24–41; my discussion of "Indian Policy in Early Virginia," *ibid.*, I (1944), 65–82; and Robert H. Land, "Henrico and Its College," *ibid.*, 2d ser., XVIII (1938), 453–98.

36. Nancy Lurie's "Indian Cultural Adjustment," is especially helpful. Although the discussion is general, it is built primarily around the story of Virginia's Indians.

37. Barbour, *Jamestown Voyages*, II, 262–63; Hulton and Quinn, *American Drawings of John White* for an example of their work in pottery; and Thomas Hariot's comparison of it with the best in England in Quinn, *Roanoke Voyages*, I, 437.

38. Quinn, *Roanoke Voyages*, I, 277.

39. Kingsbury, *Records of the Virginia Company*, III, 14–15.

40. Strachey, *Historie of Travell*, pp. 90, 104–5.

41. Kingsbury, *Records of the Virginia Company*, III, 546.

42. *Ibid.*, III, 555.

43. *Ibid.*, III, 683.

44. In addition to works previously cited, see William S. Powell, "Aftermath of the Massacre: The First Indian War, 1622–1632," *Virginia Magazine of History and Biography*, LXVI (1958), 44–75.

45. Beverley, *History*, p. 62; Richard L. Morton, *Colonial Virginia* (Chapel Hill, N.C., 1960), I, 153–56. Little actually is known of the second massacre. April 18 is the date usually used because the assembly in 1645 proclaimed it a day of thanksgiving for the colony's deliverance, as had been done with March 22 after the first massacre. Governor Berkeley's absence from the colony between June 1644 and June 1645 on a trip to England has been interpreted as a trip made in search of help for the colony, but in the present state of the record it could be read to mean that the situation quickly became well enough in hand to permit the trip, whatever may have been its purpose.

46. William W. Hening, *The Statutes at Large . . . of Virginia* (Richmond, etc., 1810–23), I, 293–94, 315, 326–27.

47. *Ibid.*, I, 317–19.

48. Two informed discussions are W. Stitt Robinson, "Tributary Indians in Colonial Virginia," *Virginia Magazine of History and Biography*, LXVII (1959), 49–64; and "The Legal Status of the Indian in Colonial Virginia," *ibid.*, LXI (1953), 247–59. References found in the earlier records of the colony to tributary payments seem to refer to the agreement with the Chickahominy after 1614 for annual payments to be made on the promise of a specified number of hatchets in return.

49. Hening, *Statutes*, I, 323–26 .

50. In *A Perfect Description of Virginia*, reprinted in *Virginia Historical Register*, II (1849), 73.

51. It has been said that Totopotomoi, chief of the Pamunkeys at the

time of his death midway through the 1650s, was Necotowance's successor, and possibly he was but also possibly only as chief of the Pamunkeys. The famous Queen of the Pamunkeys, who apparently succeeded Totopotomoi, seems never to have been known by any other title.

52. See, for example, the order of a general assembly in 1663 that "each perticular River" bear its own charges, "A generall warr excepted," in H. R. McIlwaine, *Journal of the House of Burgesses, 1660–1693* (Richmond, Va., 1914), p. 28.

53. A subject I have discussed in the later pages of my "Indian Policy in Early Virginia."

54. Hening, *Statutes*, II, 219.

55. *Ibid.*, II, 274–76.

56. John R. Swanton, *The Indian Tribes of North America* (Washington, 1952), p. 71.

57. *Ibid.*, pp. 63, 64, for the identification of the Men Heyricks and Manachees as the Meherrins and the Monacans.

58. Hening, *Statutes*, I, 402–3; Lurie, "Indian Cultural Adjustment" p. 54; McCary, *Indians in Seventeenth-Century Virginia*, p. 81.

59. See especially David I. Bushnell, Jr., *The Manahoac Tribes in Virginia, 1608*, in *Smithsonian Miscellaneous Collections*, 94 (1935), No. 8; and his *The Five Monacan Towns in Virginia, 1607*, *ibid.*, 82 (1930), No. 12. For the treaty and its signatories, *Virginia Magazine of History and Biography*, XIV (1907), 289–97.

60. For example, see Hening, *Statutes*, II, 138–43, 149, 150, 153, 193–94, 218–19, which together indicate that the problem was by no means limited to the consequences of intrusions by outsiders. See *ibid.*, II, 185, 202, for evidence that seemingly less serious difficulties on the south side of the James were blamed on the Tuscororas of Carolina. And for evidence of continuing difficulty on the northern frontier, see Thomas H. Warner, *History of Old Rappahannock County, Virginia, 1656–1692* (Tappahannock, Va., 1965), pp. 48–49.

61. Perhaps no more of the details can be found in any one place than in [Fairfax Harrison], *Landmarks of Old Prince William* (Richmond, 1924).

62. An overall account is George T. Hunt, *The Wars of the Iroquois: A Study in Intertribal Relations* (Madison, 1940), which should be used in consultation also with the previously cited study by Trelease.

63. See Bushnell, *Manahoac Tribes.*

64. Charles M. Andrews, *Narratives of the Insurrections* (New York, 1915), pp. 123–28.

65. See Harrison's *Landmarks of Old Prince William*, p. 194, where he declares that the Virginia government suspended the grant of patents in the area of the proprietorship in 1677, and that "there ensued an interval of twenty years during which Stafford [County] practically stood still so far as concerned new seatings."

66. See for example the petition for assistance from the king in 1682, McIlwaine, *Journal of the House of Burgesses, 1660–1693*, p. 159, where

it is affirmed that the loyalty of the friendly Indians depended on the protection that could be given them against the Senecas.

67. See especially Harrison's *Landmarks of Old Prince William*, pp. 77–88.

68. *Calendar of State Papers, Colonial, 1696–97*, p. 456.

69. See Hening, *Statutes*, I, 410, 415.

70. *William and Mary Quarterly*, 2d ser., XX (1940), 69.

71. See later depositions regarding the movements of some of the Indians after the massacre of 1644, in *Virginia Magazine of History and Biography*, VII (1900), 349–52; and a petition of 1689 from three chieftains "of the poore and distressed Remnant" of the Chickahominys, for protection against the murderous designs of other Indians with whom they had been forced to take a temporary residence by the "Rabid Hostility of the Senecas," in *Calendar of Virginia State Papers*, I, 22.

72. Blanton, *Medicine in Virginia in the Seventeenth Century* (Richmond, Va., 1930), pp. 60–61; Beverley, *History*, p. 232.

73. *Ibid.*, p. 217; Edmund and Dorothy Smith Berkeley, *The Reverend John Clayton, a Parson with a Scientific Mind: His Scientific Writings and Other Related Papers* (Charlottesville, Va., 1965), pp. 22–39.

74. See sources cited in note 60 above. I have a brief discussion of the general subject in *The Colonies in Transition, 1660–1713* (New York, 1968), pp. 112–16.

BLACK

NY transition from the subject of the Indian to that of the Negro in seventeenth-century Virginia immediately raises a question as to why the one was enslaved and the other not. Both were regarded by the English colonists as basically barbarous and savage. Each in physical appearance differed markedly from the white settler. Both were heathen, speaking generally, and so possessd of an identification providing the easiest of justifications for their enslavement. There were, it is true, a few Indian slaves in the colony, as there were also a number of Negroes who escaped enslavement. But the common experience of the two peoples was quite different in this regard.

The usual explanation for this difference depends first upon an assumption that the Indian was difficult to enslave, an assumption that may depend too much upon the old notion that the Negro was perculiarly fitted for the role, but it has to be agreed that the Indian enjoyed a decided advantage from being in his own country. When it is remembered, however, that South Carolina at the beginning of the eighteenth century had several hundred Indian slaves, possibly as much as a third of its total slave population, one begins to wonder if the answer to the question can be quite so simple.[1] South Carolina had acquired its Indian slaves as a regular item of exchange in its far-flung trade with the southeastern Indian nations. These nations had their own differences, their own wars with one another, conflicts which undoubtedly were intensified by the opportunity to sell prisoners taken in war to the Charles Town traders. It was a development comparable to that which in Africa served the demands of the trans-Atlantic slave trade. It also was a de-

velopment virtually unique in the history of the English
colonies of North America, but nevertheless one that em-
phasizes the need to pay attention to the special circumstances of time and place that in other areas may have
determined the end result.

Among such circumstances in the case of Virginia, first
mention belongs to the protection the Indian enjoyed
through the commitment the Virginia Company had made
to accomplish his salvation. However justified the modern
student may be in viewing this commitment with cynicism,
there is no escape from the fact that the promotional efforts
upon which the entire venture depended for support, finan-
cial and other, leaned heavily upon that promise. Any enslavement of Indians could have met with embarrassing
demands for explanation in England, and in a number of
very high places. After 1622, the fear and hatred of the Indian
by the settler undoubtedly deserves the chief emphasis. A
people determined to exclude all Indians from the area
of settlement were hardly in a mood to include many of
them in their own households. The decision to ship prisoners
of war out of the colony in 1645 was justified on purely
military grounds, but certainly there was another consideration.[2] The exception made for prisoners under twelve,
together with a provision in the treaty of 1646 for placing
Indian children not over that age in English households,
with the parent's consent, can be viewed with suspicion that
the arrangement might easily lead to the child's ultimate
enslavement. Supporting that view is subsequent legislation
seeking to guarantee that the child would not be enslaved,
but perhaps the need for such legislation deserves no more
emphasis than does the guarantee thus given.[3]

After mid-century, one has to keep in mind the distinction
between Virginia's own Indians, now tributary, and the outsiders, the foreign Indians. That the colonists were not
averse to imposing upon the latter a condition of servitude
approaching enslavement is suggested by Berkeley's advice

in 1666 to the militia command in the northern counties
that the cost of a campaign against the "Northern" Indians
might be defrayed by the women and children taken as
"booty."[4] There is evidence also that Virginia's traders,
pressing their trade in a southwesterly direction into an area
soon to be more fully exploited by the Charles Town traders, may have been beginning at about this time to bring
Indians purchased from other Indians into the colony for
sale.[5] But not until 1676, in one of Bacon's Laws, did the
enslavement of Indians receive a positive sanction from
public law (in the case of those seized as prisoners of war),
and that sanction lasted only for a few years.[6] In the long run,
the critical consideration would appear to be the fact that
the troublesome Indians continued to be intruders from the
north, whose enslavement could have complicated the colony's relations with other provinces, or even with a government in England increasingly alert to the role that might
be played by the Iroquois in the struggle with France. As
Virginia wisely turned to diplomacy in its search for security,
the Negroes came dangerously close to being the only people
in the colony with whom the institution of slavery was
identified.

The problem of the Negro's enslavement remains a difficult one, very largely because it was first accomplished
through custom and usage rather than by legislation. Recently, however, the difficulty has been greatly reduced, as
must be much of the controversy that has surrounded the
question, by the publication of Winthrop Jordan's penetrat-
ing study of American attitudes toward the Negro.[7] His study
reveals with new force, and with new evidence, the peculiar
vulnerability of the Negro to enslavement by the colonists.
In addition, it reinforces the evidence, unfortunately still
fragmentary, which argues that in all areas of English colonization the status of a slave, however imperfectly defined
as yet, was becoming by the 1640s the normal lot of the
Negro. I have thought it unnecessary here to renew the

discussion of this question, or to review again the successive laws enacted by the Virginia assembly after 1660 for the purpose of resolving specific problems arising from the existence of a state of enslavement for a large part, though by no means all, of the colony's Negro population. Instead, let me refer you to Professor Jordan's persuasive discussion of the subject under what has seemed to me an especially apt caption: "The Unthinking Decision."

In passing, let me also refer to two other distinguished works of recent date which bear less directly on the origins of slavery in Virginia but certainly lend a helpful perspective for such further investigation of the subject as may be undertaken. David Brion Davis in *The Problem of Slavery in Western Culture* has not attempted to write a history of slavery as such, but in an unusually well-informed discussion of the institution as it developed in different parts of America he has called into question the frequently popular view that an especially harsh form of slavery was found in the English colonies of North America.[8] Still more recently, Philip Curtin, in the first sophisticated effort to provide a comprehensive analysis of the admittedly imperfect statistical data that has survived for study of the trans-Atlantic slave trade, has presented results which put the question even more insistently.[9]

In my own review of the literature, old and new, I have been struck by the thought that American historians have been so largely concerned with the question of the Negro's status, with the origins of the institution of slavery, as to be indifferent to other questions they might have investigated. Let me hasten to insist that this remark is in no way prefatory to an announcement of some startling discovery. The plain fact is that the surviving record is so incomplete as to impose a decided limit on what we are ever likely to know about the Negro in seventeenth-century Virginia, free or slave. What bothers me is that we may have been too content to have it this way. I am speaking, in other words, of an attitude, one that seems to have been shared by black and white historians alike.

For example, our textbooks consistently assure us—as also do more specialized works by well-informed scholars—that the well-known Dutch shipmaster in 1619 brought to Virginia twenty Negroes. Most commonly, it is said that he brought them to Jamestown. In actual fact, we have no certain knowledge as to the number of these persons, and no certain documentary evidence that they were carried to Jamestown at all. Our textbooks say there were twenty because this is what Captain John Smith said in his *Historie*.[10] Robert Beverley picked up the item from Smith, added the information that these were the first to be "carried into the Country," and so began the history of one of those historical facts that become in time so well established that no author bothers to burden his text with a footnote.[11] Fortunately, the captain had a way very often of citing his source, which in this instance was a letter from John Rolfe to Sir Edwin Sandys, and not only has the original survived but for nearly forty years now its text has been readily available for consultation in any library possessing the third volume of Susan Kingsbury's *Records of the Virginia Company*.[12] There one finds instead of the "twenty Negars," as Smith paraphrased his source, a statement that there were "20. and odd Negroes." Although this is a good example of the imprecision with which a man in the seventeenth century might present such information, the Oxford *Dictionary* leaves no room for doubt that the phrasing must be read to mean somewhat more than twenty. Whether it can be read as twenty-one, twenty-two, or even more is a question that has to be left to conjecture.

There is, it is true, additional evidence, that found in the census of 1625, but this evidence hardly can be said to resolve the problem. According to the census, which was remarkably detailed, there were then living in the colony a total of twenty-three Negroes, of whom two were children

presumably born in the colony. Four of the twenty-one
adults, two men and two women, are listed as having migrated to the colony after 1619, the earliest in 1621, another
in 1622, and two as recently as 1623.[13] Only in these four
instances is the time of arrival in the colony given for the
Negroes listed, and so the remaining seventeen presumably
represent the original group. Whether this means that John
Rolfe's report of the number was mistaken, or whether several Negroes meanwhile had died, cannot be said. There is
a record of the death of one Negro at some time after April
1623, but I know of no other evidence bearing on the point.[14]

In view of the extraordinary effort that has been devoted
to the search for every discoverable detail regarding the
Susan Constant, or the *Mayflower* and its passengers, we
should perhaps turn back to Rolfe's letter for such additional
information as it provides. It was written three months or
more after the Dutchman's arrival "about the latter end
of August" at Point Comfort. There is no mention whatsoever of the ship's going up to Jamestown. The letter de-
scribes the vessel as a man-of-war of 160 tons, names the
commander as a Captain Jope, identifies the pilot as an Englishman named "Mr. Marmaduke," and reports that the ship
had been engaged in a none-too-successful plundering expe-
dition in the West Indies. It is in this connection that Rolfe
gives the number, declaring that the captain had brought
into Point Comfort "not any thing but 20. and odd Negroes."
His presence in Virginia, as also perhaps the fact that he
had an English pilot aboard, is explained by a meeting in
the West Indies between the Dutch ship and an English
vessel named the *Treasurer,* which had sailed from Virginia
for the West Indies earlier in the year and which belonged
to the Earl of Warwick, a leading Virginia and Bermuda
adventurer who probably was the heaviest English investor of
his day in privateering voyages. It had been agreed that the
two ships, both evidently short of provisions, would sail together for Virginia. According to Rolfe, they had been sep-

arated in the passage, and the *Treasurer* had come into Point
Comfort three or four days after the Dutchman dropped an-
chor there. One other important item is included in the
letter. Captain Jope had received the supplies he needed
through a sale of the Negroes to Governor Yeardley and the
Cape Merchant, resident agent or factor for administration
of the company's monopoly of the colony's trade, a post then
held by Abraham Piersey. Whether the purchase was negotiated by the two men in their public or private capacities
is not stated. It can only be reported that the census of 1625
shows eight Negroes among the servants of Sir George
Yeardley, who no longer was governor; seven among Abraham Piersey's servants, one of them a child; and two adults,
together with one infant, belonging to William Tucker, who
in 1619 happened to be the commander at Point Comfort.[15]

That Rolfe could have been wrong in some of his state-
ments is indicated by one other document, apparently the
only other surviving one to make reference to the Dutchman's
visit. It is a letter written by John Pory, possibly to the Earl
of Southampton, that was dated at Jamestown on September
30, 1619 for dispatch by way of a "man of warre of Flushing"
then on the point of sailing for London.[16] There is no question as to the identity of the vessel, for Pory explains its
presence in Virginia as the result of "an accidental consort-
ship in the West Indies" with the *Treasurer*. In closing the
letter, he states that it is being entrusted to the ship's pilot,
an Englishman named Marmaduke Rayner, who surely must
have been Rolfe's "Mr. Marmaduke." Unfortunately, Pory
found no occasion to mention the Negroes, or perhaps he
deliberately avoided mentioning the subject, and so we are
left entirely dependent upon Rolfe's account of the transaction except for a more specific identification of the ship,
the presumably correct or full name of its English pilot,
confirmation for the approximate time of the sale, and the
possibility, though no more than a possibility, that it may
actually have occurred at Jamestown.

The number of Negroes settled in Virginia in 1619 could have been much larger, for the *Treasurer* had reached Point Comfort with at least fourteen aboard. But the treatment given its master, Captain Daniel Elfrith, was quite different from that accorded the Dutch shipmaster. The leaders of the Virginia Company had become alarmed lest reports of Elfrith's use of the colony for privateering against the Spaniard 'bring upon the company the king's displeasure, and there can be no doubt that instructions from London explain the denial to Elfrith of the assistance he needed. He promptly sailed for Bermuda, where he arrived with his ship reportedly in terrible condition and with fourteen Negroes.[17] This part of the story needs mention here for more than one reason. First, some historians have assumed that Elfrith may have disposed of one or more of his Negroes before sailing for Bermuda, which seems to be very doubtful indeed. Secondly, it may help to provide a warning against the error, of which many writers have been guilty, in speaking of the Negroes carried to Virginia by the Dutchman as the first in an English colony. Actually, Elfrith's arrival in Bermuda brought the total number of Negroes in that colony to perhaps thirty, or possibly even more, and the first of them had come as early as 1616.[18] Finally, we might know more about this historic development in Virginia had not the courtesies extended to the Dutch shipmaster come very close to raising precisely the same issue as did Elfrith's presence there—the encouragement of privateering against the Spaniard. It was a very hot issue among the adventurers at the time, one contributing greatly to the bitter factional strife which helped ultimately to destroy the Virginia Company itself. Here, in other words, was a subject calling for discretion in reports to London.

On the question of the origins of Virginia's first Negro inhabitants, there is little room for doubt that they came from some part of the Spanish territories lying in or around the Caribbean.[19] This was the favored hunting ground for privateers, an area where there were thousands of miles of unprotected coastlines, where communications along the coasts or between the islands depended upon small craft, where many outlying settlements were poorly prepared to defend themselves against forces landed from hostile ships, and where Spaniards could be found who were ready enough to engage in a contraband trade.[20] John Rolfe's letter clearly indicates that the Negroes had been acquired in the West Indies, and such a conclusion is reinforced by unmistakable evidence as to the West Indian origins of most of the Negroes previously settled in Bermuda, and by a number of Spanish names among the few Negroes listed by name in the census of 1625. The conclusion naturally has led to a good deal of interesting speculation. I am myself persuaded that these people probably were native to America. It is possible that some or all of them were Christian, a possibility usually brought into discussions of the origins of the colony's free Negro population. But these are questions, like the question of their status in the colony, on which we really have no information to guide us.[21]

I know of only one other recorded instance of a Negro who definitely was brought to Virginia from the West Indies by privateers, in this case by the English crew of a captured Spanish frigate in 1625.[22] But it has to be remembered that for another quarter century and more English privateers continued to be active in that area. A main center of their activity after 1635 became the Puritan settlement of Providence Island, off the Mosquito coast of Central America, which until its seizure by the Spaniards in 1641 served as a base both for plundering expeditions and for an extensive contraband trade with Spanish territories. The Puritan colony acquired a substantial Negro population and exported Negroes as an important item in its trade with other English plantations.[23] Some of those exported could have been sent to Virginia, as some of those traded to other plantations could have reached Virginia at a later time in a remigration of their masters to the mainland.[24]

Still another instance in which a privateer may have been responsible for the importation of Negroes into the colony requires mention because it has gotten into the literature as the earliest occasion on which Africans were brought more or less directly from Africa to Virginia. The evidence is found in two letters from a local official in England reporting to his superiors in May 1628 that a Captain Arthur Guy had seized "an Angola man with many Negroes," that these had been sold in Virginia, and that the proceeds of the sale to the extent of eighty-five hogsheads and more of tobacco had been brought into Cowes.[25] Whether the transaction took place in 1627 or early 1628 is uncertain. We can be certain only that the date was not 1629, as it usually is given, and that the captain's name was not Grey, as through an apparent error of transcription it often has been rendered. There is some reason for doubting that the sale actually was made in Virginia, for Englishmen at the time could still use its name to comprehend almost any part of America not occupied by Spaniards, and by 1628 there were several English colonies, in addition to Virginia, producing tobacco in significant quantities. The colony's records indicate that a shipmaster whose name may have been Arthur Guy sailed from Virginia for London late in 1627.[26] It is quite possible that Guy delivered a number of Africans to Virginia in that year, but it can be doubted that a truly large shipment of that kind could have been received without leaving some other trace, somewhere in the surviving records, incomplete as they are.

So incomplete, to the very end of the century, is the record we have for study of the black migration to Virginia that I have decided once more to assume the risk of seeing what assistance a closer view of the land patents might provide. As with the white migration, so with the black these patents constitute the only surviving record that has any claim whatsoever to being comprehensive. From 1635 to 1699, when Governor Francis Nicholson put an end to the practice, it was policy to grant for any Negro brought into the colony the same headright of fifty acres that was awarded for the importation of other persons. Fortunately, until quite late in the century the clerks obviously made it a point to identify a Negro as a Negro, either by coupling his name with that designation, or in patents granted for unnamed persons, by specifying that a certain number of the headrights were for Negroes.* In the last quarter of the century, whether through carelessness, or to save time, or because the requirement that headrights be listed by name was more consistently observed than it had been before, the identification of the person as a Negro was often omitted, especially after 1690.† Even so, there is no real difficulty in identifying the Negroes, who regularly were listed by a single name, usually one the earlier part of the record has shown to be in common use for Negroes, whereas other headrights were listed by their Christian and family names. All told, by my rough count, 4,068 headrights were recorded for persons identifiable as Negroes.

I have no intention of suggesting for a moment that this figure, or others shortly to be presented, can be considered precise. In some patents the Negroes are helpfully grouped together; in many other instances they are scattered through the list of headrights in such a way as to require that every list be scanned for the purpose of identifying them. Not only

* Confirmation for the belief that this was a consistently maintained practice is found in the very evident inclination of the clerks to distinguish in a similar way other immigrants who were not English, including the Scotch, Irish, and at times the Welsh. The usage is more noticeable in the case of the Negroes mainly because there were so many more of them.

† Perhaps the more frequent use of names toward the end of the century has its explanation in a new care to observe at least one of the requirements at a time when the administration of the system was being increasingly corrupted.

may I have been guilty of an occasional oversight, but it seems reasonable to assume that the abusive usages which are known to have corrupted the record generally were also operative in claims made for the importation of Negroes.* It cannot be determined whether the fact that the Negro belonged to a very special category among the persons entering the colony had the effect of making the record for the black migration either more or less complete than for the white. There are difficulties, but it is a record which at the least may serve to raise certain questions that perhaps require reexamination of long-standing assumptions.

Unfortunately, the land patents normally carry no fuller information for the black immigrants than they do for the white as to the place from which they came or the time of their arrival in the colony. But there are helpful indications, which on occasion can be strengthened by reference to other evidence. There are, for example, the names by which Negroes were listed. It has to be admitted that these names often tell us much more about the men who gave them, doubtless at times under some pressure for immediate conformity with the requirement that headrights be recorded by name, than about the persons who bore them. The crude humor with which shipmasters or purchasers drew upon ancient history or mythology for the names of Caesar, Hannibal, Nero, Jupiter, Pluto, or Minerva; the Primus and Secundus who headed one list; and the use more than once of Ape or Monkey for a name records principally an all-too-prevalent attitude of the white toward the black. On the other hand, the frequent recurrence until well past mid-century of Spanish or Portuguese names—such names as Francisco, Pedro, Antonio, Isabella, Angelo, Domingo, and its contraction Mingo—strongly suggests that the Caribbean continued

* Because I previously have explained what the faults in the record may be, let me add here no more than a reminder that the figures for the later years of the century are evidently the ones most open to question. See below, pp. 11–13, 17.

through many years to be an important area of recruitment, however direct or indirect may have been the route followed from Spanish territories to Virginia.[27]

Although, as with the full migration, no close correlation can be assumed between the time of a person's arrival in the colony and the date of his appearance as a headright in a land patent, the distribution of Negro headrights over the larger spans of time have an obvious significance. Thus, by my count, there were 140 such headrights recorded from 1635 through 1639. It cannot be concluded that this many Negroes entered the colony during those five years, for it will be remembered that the years immediately following the king's clarification of policy in 1634 was a time for catching up on a backlog of claims. But the figure certainly provides some indication of the number brought into the colony between 1625 and 1640. No less interesting is the evidence that the decade of the 1640s saw a decided drop in the number imported. Land patents issued in 1640 carried only one black headright, in two other years (1644 and 1646) there were none at all, and the total for the decade of the 1640s comes to no more than 105, of which total almost half belongs to the single year of 1649. The number of black headrights recorded in the 1650s climbs to 317, bringing the sum total for the years before 1660 to 562.*

In 1660 the number drops from the sixteen of the preceeding year to just two. Some immediately will have thought of the frequently cited patent granted Richard Lee in No-

* The headrights were distributed as follows:

1635:	26	1640:	1	1650:	11
1636:	10	1641:	7	1651:	35
1637:	29	1642:	23	1652:	53
1638:	59	1643:	10	1653:	32
1639:	16	1644:	0	1654:	31
		1645:	4	1655:	4
		1646:	0	1656:	68
		1647:	7	1657:	31
		1648:	2	1658:	36
		1649:	51	1659:	16

vember of that year for the transportation of eighty Negroes, but there is good reason for believing that none of these persons reached Virginia. The evidence is found in a grant of November 29, 1667 to Henry Corbyn, which included, by special order of the governor and council, headrights for thirty-six persons lost at sea on their way to Virginia, and it is stated in the patent that the precedent for this action was the benefit "in the like kind" enjoyed by Colonel Lee under a special order of the Quarter Court dated October 18, 1660.[28] At the time there was only one Colonel Lee in Virginia, and there is no record of any other patent granted to Richard Lee in that year.[29]

Accordingly, I have omitted Lee's eighty headrights in a count that brings the total for the 1660s to 609, a figure that falls a little short of doubling the total for the 1650s. The count for the first half of the 1670s suggests that the migration continued at approximately the rate established in the preceding decade, which is to say at an average of about sixty per year, but after 1674 the numbers decline and the total for the ten years falls to no more than 421. In the 1680s the sum total is 629. For the 1690s it is 1,847.*

Let me say at once that there are difficulties in interpreting the figures just given for the last quarter of the century, and especially those for its last two decades. The possible exaggeration of the overall total, as a result of the especially abusive usages known to have characterized the administration of the system in the later years of the century, presents

* The count by year is as follows:

1660:	2	1670:	33	1680:	37	1690:	182
1661:	69	1671:	51	1681:	23	1691:	234
1662:	53	1672:	51	1682:	172	1692:	44
1663:	79	1673:	57	1683:	102	1693:	142
1664:	77	1674:	104	1684:	54	1694:	202
1665:	144	1675:	33	1685:	1	1695:	305
1666:	110	1676:	28	1686:	7	1696:	258
1667:	27	1677:	2	1687:	95	1697:	201
1668:	18	1678:	42	1688:	73	1698:	246
1669:	30	1679:	20	1689:	65	1699:	33

less of a problem than does evidence which calls into question the distribution of headrights within the period. These were years in which the Royal African Company, chartered in 1672, was greatly expanding England's share of the slave trade. Unfortunately, its records provide no answer to the question of how many Africans it may have delivered to Virginia, as Kenneth Davies's informed history of the company advises us, but that study also indicates that in the period ending with the company's loss of its monopoly in 1698 no deliveries were made to Virginia after 1689.[30] The fragmentary evidence included in Elizabeth Donnan's previously published collection of documents illustrative of the slave trade points to the same conclusion, and suggests the possibility that shipments to Virginia through the company's agencies between 1678 and 1686 could have been in the neighborhood of nine hundred.[31] Even more uncertain is the number of Africans who may have been brought to the colony by interlopers, who by 1698 had become politically powerful enough to bring an end to the company's monopoly through an act of parliament. But the one documented instance of interloping activity we have falls in 1687, when a Bristol ship ran aground on the Eastern Shore with an obviously illegal cargo of 120 Negroes.[32] Incomplete and uncertain as the evidence is, it argues that the headrights recorded during the decade, and perhaps a little more, immediately preceding 1690 probably represent an understatement of the actual number of Negroes brought to the colony at that time. And this, in turn, raises the question of whether the greatly expanded number of black headrights in the 1690s actually reflects the scale of the migration in that decade, or whether it is substantially representative of postponed claims for Negroes reaching the colony somewhat earlier.

I am inclined to believe that the latter was the case, that the importations of the 1690s actually may have been less impressive than historians long have thought because of the

very great increase in the number of black headrights recorded in that decade. Such a view is reinforced by the
known disruptions of the normal channels of trade, both
with Africa and Virginia, occasioned during the first half of
the decade by the war with France. I am unable to offer a
fully satisfactory explanation for what appear to be decisions
to defer making claims for some of the Negroes imported in
the preceding decade, but two suggestions may be helpful.
The Royal African Company enjoyed the consistently strong
patronage of the last two Stuart kings, who strictly instructed
their governors to lend every assistance to the company in
upholding its monopoly. With Lord Howard of Effingham,
a man noted for following instructions, serving as governor
for almost five years after 1684, it could have been the better
part of wisdom for a planter who had purchased Africans
from an interloper to postpone the revelation that might be
involved in securing a land patent. After 1689 the attitude
of King William's government, and of the company itself,
was more tolerant of interloping.[33] Of greater importance
may have been the special fee of two hundred pounds of
tobacco imposed by Effingham, beginning in the spring of
1685, upon every use of the colony's seal on a land patent,
as on other documents. Perhaps the House of Burgesses, in
its later indictment of the governor, was quite correct when
it charged that the fee had deterred many men from use of
the seal for taking up land. The fee was discontinued in
1689.[34]

With the exception of an apparent need for some redistri-
bution of headrights in the later years of the century, I have
found no reason for doubting that the record provided by
the land patents is reasonably, though roughly, indicative of
the black migration into seventeenth-century Virginia. The
totals for any year or other period of time, except probably
for the decade of the 1680s, may well be too large, for as with
the white headrights it has to be assumed that there was
some duplication of claims. But I am fully persuaded, for ex-

ample, that a considerably larger number of Negroes was brought to Virginia during the fifteen years beginning with 1660 than had been brought through the entire period preceding that year.

If I am at all correct, the chief among time-honored assumptions to be called into question is the belief that at mid-century Dutch merchants, trading in the Chesapeake with greater freedom than they theretofore had enjoyed or thereafter would be allowed, impressively enlarged the colony's black labor force. It is quite possible that the Dutch were the chief source of supply at that time, but it would appear that the number they supplied can be easily exaggerated. There seems to be a general agreement that Dutch shipmasters enjoyed their greatest freedom of trade with Virginia during the twelve years preceding the colony's surrender to Cromwell and the outbreak of the first Anglo-Dutch war in 1652.[35] At the end of that year, however, the total number of Negroes listed as headrights since 1640 barely exceeded 200, with 150 of this total belonging to the four years beginning with 1649.* Evidently the Dutch, then heavily engaged in underwriting the conversion from tobacco to sugar and from white labor to black labor in the English West Indian plantations, had few Negroes left for shipment to Virginia.

By the same token it has to be suggested that English slave traders were comparably indifferent to the market in Virginia at this time. We know very little about the English trade with Africa before the Restoration, indeed before the chartering of the Royal African Company in 1672, and what we know indicates that the trade was slow to develop and also slow to give the slave trade a high priority among its objectives.[36] But recently Professor Brenner has discovered evidence that the "new merchants," those building their fortunes upon a trade with the American plantations, were

* See table on p. 85.

leaders in the development of a serious English interest in
the slave trade, that for the most part they traded at first as
interlopers challenging the monopoly of the Guinea Company, and that this challenge was beginning to assume
serious proportions by the late 1630s.[37] The evidence supporting this view includes a patent for three thousand acres
received in the spring of 1638 by George Menefie, merchant,
planter, and member of the governor's council in Virginia.
Among the sixty headrights were twenty-three Negroes described simply as the "Negroes I brought out of England
with me."[38] It is possible that this was the first shipment of
Africans to reach Virginia without stop or stay in some
other part of America. Whatever may be the fact on that
point, the suggestion that they had been acquired from some
English slave trader is unmistakable, and it is known that
Menefie had connections in the amorphous group of "new
merchants." It is also known that he was in London as late
as July of the preceding year.[39] He returned to London in
1638 on a commission to recruit craftsmen for building a
statehouse at Jamestown, and so the fifteen unnamed Negroes
included as headrights in another patent for three thousand
acres he secured in 1639 possibly also came from Africa by
way of England.[40]

For merchants trading chiefly with the American plantations the slave trade was a natural development of their
primary interest, and such men as Maurice Thompson seem
to have come out of the disruptions of the English Civil
War with a heightened interest in that trade. But there can
be little doubt that their chief hope was to overcome the
decided lead the Dutch had taken as underwriters of the
sugar boom in the West Indies. We have no certain statistical
evidence as to the scale of the slave trade to the West Indian
plantations at mid-century, but estimates that have been
made suggest that annual importations into Barbados may
have run well above a thousand from early in the 1640s,
and may have reached the level of two thousand before

1650.[41] By comparison the some three hundred Negroes who presumably entered Virginia during the following decade are a small number indeed.

If we may trust the evidence offered by the land patents, the largest importers of Negroes into Virginia before the 1660s were themselves Virginia planters, or perhaps I should say merchant-planters. The twenty-three Negroes brought from England by George Menefie in 1638 remained the largest number recorded in a single patent before 1656, when a patent granted two daughters of Edmund Scarborough, leading planter and merchant on the Eastern Shore, included forty-one Negroes among the seventy headrights listed.[42] One looks a second time at this patent, for most of the names of the additional headrights are so obviously Irish as to suggest that all had been shipped together from Britain. But it is known that Scarborough had been in New Amsterdam the preceding August, where before sailing for Virginia with an unspecified number of "purchased Negroes," he gave bond not to enter Delaware Bay or River on his way home. Thus, it can be concluded that the forty-one Negroes represent this purchase or a part of it. I say part because two other patents bearing the same date as that issued to his daughters included as headrights a total of ten Negroes who had been assigned to the patentees by Scarborough.[43] It is possible that Scarborough was responsible for the largest single shipment into Virginia of Negroes whose presence in America is presumably attributable to the Dutch slave trade.

Unfortunately, there appears to be no clue as to where Richard Lee may have secured the eighty Negroes for whom, despite their apparent loss at sea, he received a patent for four thousand acres in the fall of 1660. It can only be said that he had a close business connection in London with John Jeffreys, twelve years later a charter member of the Royal African Company and founder of a mercantile house which toward the end of the century, under the leadership of the founder's nephew, would be especially active in supplying African laborers for Virginia.[44] Although I have omitted these eighty headrights from my tabulations, Lee's patent remains one of extraordinary historical interest. Not until the 1690s is there found a patent listing a larger number of Negroes, and even then there were only four such patents.[45] The document, moreover, is unique among patents issued before the final quarter of the century in being granted for Negro headrights exclusively. When placed alongside the Menefie and Scarborough patents, it reinforces a suggestion that the Virginia planters were prompt in recognizing the advantages of Negro labor.

That this awareness was by no means restricted to a few planters is indicated by the frequently cited statute of March 1660 which offered to Dutch merchants bringing in "Negro slaves" exemption from an export duty imposed two years earlier upon tobacco shipped out of the colony for destinations other than England.[46] The statute commonly has been cited in the context of a discussion of the Dutch supply of Negroes to Virginia at mid-century, and read as an effort by the assembly to encourage the Dutch merchants to continue the supply. But another reading, with a somewhat different emphasis, is possible. The statute was enacted at a difficult moment in the colony's history, but one that was not lacking in hopeful prospects. The bill came from the same assembly which shrewdly anticipated the course of political developments in England by electing Sir William Berkeley as governor several weeks before the restoration of Charles II to the English throne. Perhaps it can be said that the assemblymen less shrewdly anticipated the effect of that restoration upon Oliver Cromwell's colonial policy. The Navigation Act of 1660, together with the failure of Berkeley's mission of 1661–62 to win at Westminster any concession to Virginia's petition for a freer trade than that act allowed, foreclosed such prospects as may have existed for a major contribution to the colony's labor force by the Dutch.

It is not my purpose to suggest that Virginia might have made its heavy commitment to Negro labor a generation before it actually did. Although the act for the encouragement of Dutch traders was passed at a time when the migration of indentured servants was apparently in marked decline, that migration quickly returned to flood tide, indeed to the highest levels established at any time during the century. All the more interesting, therefore, is the evidence in the land patents that simultaneously the Virginians almost doubled the scale of their importations of Negro servants. It hardly can be argued that this development was attributable to a critical shortage of labor, or that trans-Atlantic slave traders were pressing the colonists to accept larger shipments, for it is well known that these traders, of whatever nationality, had little interest in markets incapable of providing ready acceptance for cargoes of one hundred to two hundred or more slaves, and in no more than three of the fifteen years following 1660 (1665, 1666, and 1674) did the grand total of headrights for Negroes exceed one hundred. What is known of the English slave trade before 1672 indicates that the West Indian plantations continued to receive an overriding priority, and how overriding that priority could be is indicated by the fact that the Royal African Company by 1689 had delivered some fifty-eight thousand slaves to the West Indies during a period in which the evidence available to us suggests that it may have sent somewhere near a thousand to Virginia.[47] The question, it appears, is where and how the Virginians managed to find the Negroes they were importing in increasing numbers.

On that question, happily, we have a helpful document, and so the kind of evidence that perhaps is still the most reassuring for most historians. It is found in a report by Edmund Jennings, acting governor of the colony, to the Board of Trade in 1708 that before 1680, according to the testimony of the older inhabitants, "what negroes were brought to Virginia were imported generally from Barbados

for it was very rare to have a Negro ship come to this Country
directly from Africa."[48] The date of the document falls a
bit late, and the testimony of older inhabitants is not always
dependable, but there are reasons other than the apparently
low level of importations before 1680 which argue that the
statement is substantially correct. The trade between Virginia and the West Indies—carried at times in shipping at
least partially owned by Virginians, but more often perhaps
by New England, Barbadian, or English ships—seems to have
been a growing one during the course of the century and
probably deserves heavier emphasis than it has generally
been given by historians.[49] Many of the English merchants
who were active in the tobacco trade continued to have in-
terests in the West Indies, and although by mid-century the
northern sailing route from England to Virginia was preferred, ships might still follow the southern route that made
a call at Barbados convenient.[50] Such evidence as we have
indicates that a call there may have been the common practice of ships delivering Africans to Virginia on contracts
between the Royal African Company and established merchants in the colony's trade, and there is also evidence that
a Virginia planter might get a share in a contract intended
perhaps for deliveries chiefly to Barbadian planters.[51] Worth
mentioning, at least, is the repeated use in headright lists
during the second half of the century of the name "Barbados
Mary." Finally, there is the well established fact that Virginia
continued through much of the eighteenth century to draw
upon the West Indies for a by-no-means insignificant proportion of the Negroes brought into the colony.[52]

No doubt there were some West Indian Negroes who migrated to Virginia with their masters, as did the original
Negro population of South Carolina, but the very scanty
evidence that is available as to the scale of that migration
makes it impossible even to guess at the number.[53] Nor is it
possible to determine how long the Negroes brought from
Barbados may have been resident in that island. Certainly

some of them only recently had arrived from Africa, but it has to be observed that until the end of the century, or very close to it, Barbados had the largest as well as one of the older Negro populations in the English plantations. There, as in no other place, was it possible to acquire slaves who had lived in an English community long enough to gain some knowledge of the language, to have made at least a partial adjustment to unfamiliar cultural patterns, and to have become acclimatized—to use the old term for what Philip Curtin recently has reminded us was a successful exposure to an "unfamiliar disease environment."[54] These are considerations which long have been used to explain in part a generally heavy dependence in New England and the other northern colonies upon Negroes imported from the West Indies,[55] and it would be difficult to argue that the planters in seventeenth-century Virginia remained indifferent to all such considerations, or to the opportunities they had for a supply from Barbados. Indeed, the land patents suggest a pattern in the importation of Negroes at this time that seems to argue the opposite.

Among the patents including headrights for black immigrants, the representative patent included one, two, three, or six and at the most eight such headrights, often listed together with other headrights in a way that invites consideration of the possibility that all belonged to the same shipment. Thus, the 562 Negroes listed as headrights before 1660 are scattered through 173 different patents, for an average of 3.2 per patent, and no more than 11 of the 173 patents included over 8 Negroes. In the 1660s, with 125 patents carrying Negro headrights, the average per patent rose to almost 4.9, and there were 22 patents which included more than 8 Negroes, but the larger listings can be considered large only in comparison with the others. Among the 22 patents listing more than 8 Negroes, the largest single claim made upon the land office for the importation of Negroes was for 25 headrights, and the average of these larger claims was less than 15.[56] Together the 22 patents account for 323 of the decade's black headrights—in other words, for the major part of the total of 609, but hardly by an impressive margin. The overall average for the 1670s fell back to 3.4, but it rose in the 1680s to 4.8, and in the final decade of the century to 7.7.

One obvious question demands immediate attention. Does the preponderance of patents listing no more than a small number of Negroes, especially noticeable through the years falling before 1680, represent the actual character of the black migration to Virginia at this time, or does it speak rather of a wide distribution of ownership through purchases made from much larger shipments? It can be agreed at once that this evidence reinforces the view that until quite late in the century the typical slaveholder possessed only a few Negroes, and that this conclusion has a very special importance. It also has to be agreed that the larger shipments probably were brought in by men who intended to place the cargoes on the market, as so often was the case with large shipments of white servants. Mention, too, should be made of evidence that contract shipments by the Royal African Company during the 1680s were commonly divided up among several planters. Perhaps earlier there were a number of shipments larger than those which found their way into the land patents, but any one who is familiar with those patents, and with the testimony they bear as to the practices followed by major importers of servants, must find it surprising that one or two of them, at least, did not get into the record. Why is it, one asks, that after the Scarborough grant of 1656 more than a quarter-century passed before another patent, with the single exception of Richard Lee's patent for a shipment evidently lost at sea, was issued listing a comparable number of Negroes? Or, why is it that not infrequently through the intervening years a patent for one hundred or more headrights, a number large enough to suggest that a claim was being made for an entire shipment of persons, included at the most three or four Negroes?[57]

These are questions more easily stated than answered. Indeed, the evidence provided by the land patents is of a kind that necessarily limits general observations regarding the origins of Virginia's Negro population to a few suggestions, but let me offer two or three. It was a very mixed population, I believe, so mixed as to make it virtually impossible to say anything more specific regarding their African provenance than that they, or their ancestors, had come chiefly at some time or other from West Africa. Perhaps this mixed character of the original population can help explain the relative indifference of Virginia planters in the eighteenth century to this question of provenance as they greatly expanded the size of their importations from Africa.[58] It is my impression that until late in the seventeenth century Virginia's Negro population had much more in common with those of the northern colonies than historians often have assumed. More than a few of these people probably were native to America, and among the natives of Africa there were some who had resided for a time in another part of America.

It is impossible to suggest what proportion of the total number entering the colony may have been brought more or less directly from Africa. If it be assumed, as possibly it can be on the testimony of the Menefie and Scarborough patents, that the larger claims upon the land office are more likely to represent this group, and if the figures given before for the 1660s be used as the test, the proportion at that time would be something like 50 percent. The proportion conceivably may have been higher in the closing years of the 1630s, for one or two patents in addition to those of George Menefie suggest that before 1641, the year usually given for the introduction of sugar into Barbados, the Virginia planter could have had as good a chance as any other to draw

upon the newly developing English slave trade.[59] Certainly
the proportion of Africans increased during the last quarter
of the century, but it should be observed that to the very
end of the century the land patents carry many indications
that small lot importations continued to represent a significant part of the migration.

The size of Virginia's Negro population at any time after
1625 remains a difficult question. An anonymous pamphlet
published at London in 1649 declared that there then were
300 Negroes in the colony,[60] and this appears to be not too far
off the mark, in view of the 245 headrights that had been
recorded by the end of that year.* On the other hand, Sir
William Berkeley's report that there were 2,000 in 1671, if
it is at all correct to assume that the headrights for this
period establish some outer limit for the actual migration,
is called into serious question. According to my count, the
grand total of black headrights through 1671 is 1,255, and
almost half of these are accounted for by patents issued within the preceding decade. Some allowance has to be made, of
course, for a natural increase, but such evidence as we have
on that subject makes it very doubtful that in 1671 there
could have been nearly 750 Negroes who were native to
Virginia. Lord Culpepper's estimate of 3,000 in 1681 also
may be open to question, but he probably was closer to the
fact than Sir William had been.

Unfortunately, the headrights provide no base for anything approaching an exact calculation of the sex ratio in
the Negro migration to seventeenth-century Virginia. Although it is possible to identify by sex more than half of the
headrights recorded, either by the name used or by some
designation of the sex when names were not listed, there is a
great difference in the percentages of the total in successive
periods of time that can be so identified. Because the names
were more frequently given in the final quarter of the cen-

---

* For the figures used here and hereafter, see tables on pp. 85 and 86.

tury, much the highest percentage of the total which is identifiable by sex falls in that period, and regrettably the lowest
percentage is that for the third quarter, a period of critical
importance for any attempt to estimate the effect of a natural
increase in the population toward the end of the century.*

Even so, suggestions that may be helpful can be drawn
from the figures. The ratio of 180.5 for the years preceding
1650, with more than 40 percent of the total of 245 headrights identifiable by sex, is close enough to the two to one
ratio that seems to have been more or less characteristic of
the slave trade to justify a suggestion that the black migration up to that time could have brought some 80 females into
the colony.† The low ratio of 159.7 for the next twenty-five
years undoubtedly needs an upward adjustment to take into
account the probabilities for the nearly 72 percent of the
total number of headrights that is not identifiable by sex. If
this adjustment were to bring the ratio up to something like
two to one, a migration of 1200 Negroes, which is the total
of black headrights for the period stated in round numbers,
would have brought into the colony approximately 400 females, most of them probably of child-bearing age. If the
actual ratio was higher than two to one, which is possible,
the number of females would be correspondingly lower. If
a further allowance be needed for duplication in headright
claims, something always to be suspected in the record we

* A tabulation, from which all names, or abbreviations of names, that
are in any way debatable have been omitted, has provided the following
data:

Total headrights		Identifiable by sex	Percentage
1635–49:	245	101	41.2
1650–74:	1,222	348	28.4
1675–99:	2,601	1,924	73.9

† The ratios for the successive periods have been calculated as
follows:

Identifiable by sex		Male	Female	Sex ratio
1635–49:	101	65	36	180.5
1650–74:	348	214	134	159.7
1675–99:	1,924	1,409	515	273.5

are using, it becomes doubtful that many more than 400 Negro women had reached Virginia by 1675. Of these, moreover, many only recently had arrived in the colony.

There would appear to be little point in continuing an exercise that can serve only to remind us that there were decided limitations imposed by the very character of the migration upon the potential for a natural increase in the colony's Negro population during the course of the seventeenth century. As during the final quarter of the century the migration grew in size, so also apparently did the ratio of male to female become higher, a development wholly consistent with the assumption that larger importations were now being made directly from Africa. A comparison with instructions from the Royal African Company to its agents in Africa will suggest that the indicated ratio of 273.5 for the last quarter of the century may be a bit high.[61] But more important perhaps is the indication that the imbalance of the sexes in the black migration to seventeenth-century Virginia apparently never became so marked as it was in the white migration to the colony.*

So far as I know, no information has been assembled on the fertility of Negro women under the conditions of life they met in seventeenth-century Virginia. Once more, it is possible only to offer a few suggestions, each of them carrying some warning of the risk that the rate of reproduction can be exaggerated. The basic consideration would appear to be a wide dispersal of ownership. The subject needs more attention than it has received, but such evidence as we have, including that in the land patents, argues that a larger proportion of the blacks experienced through most of the century a significantly higher degree of separation, or even isolation, from their fellows than later would be the case.[62] It may also be true that the modern student, following the logic of his own calculations, too readily has assumed that

* See above, pp. 26–27.

the seventeenth-century planter was prompt to recognize the advantages of a self-perpetuating labor force. The only points on which we can be certain are that the Negroes were valued at first chiefly for the longer term of their service, that the females were commonly employed in the fields, that the interruptions occasioned by pregnancy and the care of a child could be costly, and that elsewhere masters did not always encourage breeding among their slaves.[63] It may be worth recalling that the census of 1625 showed only two Negro children, despite the near balance of eleven males to ten females in an adult black population that for the most part had been resident in the colony better than five years.* Finally, one must consider the attitude of the women themselves, and especially of those freshly brought from Africa. Many comments have been made upon the morbidity, at times expressed in suicide, of the African after reaching America, and the unwillingness of some women to bring a child into the condition of enslavement.

The presence of an increasing number of mulattoes can hardly be ignored as a factor offsetting one of the influences mentioned earlier. However often Negroes in early Virginia may have been isolated from the company of their fellows, they certainly lived no less often in close and daily contact, in the field and about the house, not only with other servants but also with the master and the master's family, and this in a colony where the imbalance of the sexes was perhaps more marked than in any other of the North American settlements. Public policy from an early date, presumably because there were enough English women present to determine social conventions, discouraged miscegenation. Although a statutory prohibition of intermarriage evidently came first in an act of 1691, especially severe penalties for fornication

---

* It is of some interest to note in this connection that Abraham Piersey, one of the two chief owners of Negroes in 1625, had four men and one woman on his property, while George Yeardley held five women and three men.

involving the black and the white had been imposed as early as 1630, and after 1662 statute law established the penalty as double that for an ordinary case of fornication. Even so, nature obviously had its way. The term *mulatto* had come into use by the 1650s. Its first use in a statute seems to have been in an act of 1672 declaring all "negro and molatto children" born "in this country" tithable at the age of sixteen. Thereafter, few statutes dealing in any way with the question of the Negro departed from the standard reading of "Negroes and Mulattoes." How many of the latter there were it is impossible to say. It has been assumed that a considerable number of the colony's free Negroes were mulattoes who had achieved their freedom through manumission by their own fathers. But we actually know very little about the mulatto. It is difficult to think of a subject more neglected by historians, no doubt because custom and law had classified the mulatto as a Negro before the end of the century and so left him with no history of his own.[64]

There appears to be no reason for assuming that the Negroes in seventeenth-century Virginia suffered an excessive rate of mortality. Certainly there is no evidence of conditions comparable to those in the West Indies, where the excess of deaths over births repeatedly produced a net decrease that was balanced by fresh importations from Africa. According to Philip Alexander Bruce, the conversion to Negro labor in Virginia was encouraged by the belief that the African required no "seasoning," as so often did the white servant with a resultant loss of time due the master.[65] This quite possibly is true, for by the second half of the century malaria could well have been the disease consistently besetting the new arrival from England. It was a disease endemic to West Africa, and the African may have brought with him a degree of immunity to its worst effects not enjoyed by the servant coming from England.[66] Moreover, some of the Negroes reaching the colony from other parts of America were perhaps already "seasoned," in the sense of

having made their own adjustment to the unfamiliar diseases of European communities.

Modern estimates of the size of Virginia's Negro population at the end of the century serve chiefly to emphasize the
difficulty of the problem. They range from the estimate of
six thousand by Bruce to the sixteen thousand found in the
Historical Statistics of the United States.[67] One has to consider that well before 1700 the familiar outlines of the Virginia type of plantation were clearly emerging, with its
predominantly black labor force, its slave quarters, and its
overseers. As early as 1686 William Fitzhugh could boast
that most of the twenty-nine Negroes he then owned were
native to Virginia, and the higher valuations placed in inven-
tories of estates upon native born slaves thereafter become
noticeable.[68] But when one considers further the possibility
that the record of the black migration carried by the land
patents exaggerates its size, the several factors that could
have affected the potential for a natural increase, and the
need to find some figure that fits well with the known acceleration of importations after 1698, the weight of the argument seems to favor an estimate somewhat larger but not
greatly in excess of six thousand.[69]

In conclusion, let me say that I am painfully aware that I
have raised in these discussions many more questions than I
have been able to answer. I can only hope that you may
agree that the lecture platform is an appropriate place to
raise questions.

Notes

1. Estimates of the number of Indian slaves at that time vary. See
Verner W. Crane, *The Southern Frontier, 1670–1732* (Durham, N.C.,

1928), p. 113; and M. Eugene Sirmans, *Colonial South Carolina: A Political History* (Chapel Hill, N.C., 1966), p. 60.

2. *William and Mary Quarterly*, 2d ser., XX (1940), 69.

3. Hening, *The Statutes at Large . . . of Virginia* (Richmond, etc., 1810–23), I, 396, 455.

4. Thomas H. Warner, *History of Old Rappahannock County, Virginia, 1656–1692* (Tappahannock, Va., 1965), pp. 48–49;*William and Mary Quarterly*, 1st ser., VIII (1899), 165, where the date is given as about 1668.

5. As in the well-known statute of 1670 (Hening, *Statutes*, II, 283) declaring that "all servants not being christians imported into this colony by shipping shalbe slaves for their lives; but what shall come by land shall serve, if boyes or girles, untill thirty yeares of age, if men or women twelves yeares and no longer."

6. Hening, *Statutes*, II, 341–46; W. Stitt Robinson, Jr., "The Legal Status of the Indian in Colonial Virginia," *Virginia Magazine of History and Biography*, LXI (1953), especially pp. 254–57.

7. Winthrop D. Jordan, *White over Black: American Attitudes toward the Negro, 1550–1812* (Chapel Hill, N.C., 1968).

8. (Ithaca, N.Y., 1966), see especially pp. 223–61.

9. Philip D. Curtin, *The Atlantic Slave Trade: A Census* (Madison, Wis., 1969).

10. Edward Arber and A. G. Bradley, eds., *The Travels and Works of Captain John Smith* (Edinburgh, 1910), II, 541.

11. *The History and Present State of Virginia*, ed. Louis B. Wright (Chapel Hill, N.C., 1947), p. 48.

12. Susan M. Kingsbury, *Records of the Virginia Company of London* (Washington, 1906–35), III, 241–48.

13. Evarts B. Greene and Virginia Harrington, *American Population before the Federal Census of 1790* (New York, 1932), p. 144; John C. Hotten, The *Original Lists of Persons of Quality . . . and Others Who Went from Great Britain to the American Plantations, 1600–1700* (London, 1874), pp. 224, 241, 258.

14. *Ibid.*, p. 189.

15. *Ibid.*, pp. 217–18, 222, 244.

16. Kingsbury. *Records of the Virginia Company*, III, 219–22.

17. See Wesley Frank Craven, *Dissolution of the Virginia Company* (New York, 1932), pp. 124–39, for an account of this incident and its far-reaching consequences.

18. Wesley Frank Craven, *An Introduction to the History of Bermuda* (Williamsburg, Va., 1937–38), pp. 91–94.

19. More than one scholar has felt it advisable in this connection to mention the later prominence of the Dutch in the African slave trade, or the fact that the Earl of Warwick was a member of the recently organized English Guinea Company. Very little seems to be known of the early English and Dutch trade with Africa, but that little appears to argue against a challenge to Rolfe's statement that Jope had been acting under

"a lardge and ample" commission "to range and to take purchase in the West Indyes." As for the *Treasurer*, its movements are so well documented as virtually to preclude any possibility other than that he acquired the Negroes in the West Indies. Moreover, there is reason for believing that Warwick's membership in the Guinea Company was more formal than active, and evidence that the company itself was slow indeed to develop an interest in the slave trade. See J. W. Blake, "The Farm of the Guinea Trade," in H. A. Cronne, T. W. Moody, and D. B. Quinn, *Essays in British and Irish History in Honour of James Eadie Todd* (London, 1949), pp. 86–106.

20. See Kenneth R. Andrews, *Elizabethan Privateering: English Privateering during the Spanish War, 1585–1603* (Cambridge, 1964), pp. 159–86, for an account probably hardly less applicable to the year 1619.

21. It has been argued that the Christian names some of the Negroes bore indicate that they had been baptized, but such an assumption can hardly be viewed as conclusive. The only specific evidence bearing on the question of religion is the listing in the census of 1625 of William Tucker's Negroes as Anthony, Isabell, "and William her child," who is described as having been baptized. See Hotten, *Original Lists*, p. 244.

22. H. R. McIlwaine, *Minutes of the Council and General Court of Colonial Virginia* (Richmond, Va., 1924), pp. 67, 68, 71, 72, 73; *Calendar of State Papers, Colonial, 1578–1660*, p. 77.

23. Arthur P. Newton, *The Colonising Activities of the English Puritans* (New Haven, 1914), pp. 149–50, 213, 225, 258–61, 302.

24. Information on migration from the island plantations to Virginia is very limited, but it can be noted that there was a report as early as 1635 that 205 persons recently had come to the colony from Bermuda. Greene and Harrington, *American Population*, p. 136.

25. The letters, one dated May 13 and the other May 27, were from John Ellsey, collector of admiralty tenths for Hampshire, to Edward Nicholas, secretary to the Duke of Buckingham. *Calendar of State Papers, Domestic, 1628–1629*, pp. 110, 131, and p. 289 for letters of marque issued to "Arthur Guy and others" on July 28, 1626, for the *Fortune* of London, a vessel of 100 tons of which Guy was the master. See also *Virginia Magazine of History and Biography*, VII (1900), 265–66.

26. McIlwaine, *Minutes of the Council*, pp. 157–58, where the name is given as Arthur Guy [?], and the ship is from London, but its name apparently was unreadable in the manuscript. It should be noted that an Arthur Guy had sailed to Virginia as master of the *Warwick* of London on commission from the Virginia Company in 1621 (Kingsbury, *Records of the Virginia Company*, III, 498–501, 507). For the purpose of rounding out the record of Virginia's early Negro population, mention belongs to John Phillip, "A negro Christened in *England* 12 yeers since," who testified in an action before the governor and council in November 1624, although the testimony suggests that he may well have been a transient sailor. See McIlwaine, *Minutes of the Council*, p. 33.

27. Philip Alexander Bruce, *Economic History of Virginia in the*

Seventeenth Century (New York, 1895), II, 86–87, has a representative list of names drawn from court records as well as from land patents.

28. See in the State Library Patents No. 6, 1666–1679, Reel 5, p. 117; and in the abstracts of patents, Patent Book 6, p. 32. For Lee's patent of 1660 see Nugent, *Cavaliers and Pioneers: Abstracts of Virginia Land Grants and Patents, 1623–1800* (Richmond, 1934), p. 404, and for evidence that he sat as a member of the Quarter Court in October 1660 *Virginia Magazine of History and Biography*, XII (1904), 205. The Corbyn patent provides confirmation for the date assigned to Lee's patent, the original of which seems to have been badly mutilated, leaving the year of its granting subject to some uncertainty.

29. See Ludwell Lee Montague, "Richard Lee, the Emigrant, 1613(?)–1664" *Virginia Magazine of History and Biography*, LXII (1954), 3–49.

30. Kenneth G. Davies, *The Royal African Company* (London, 1957), pp. 294–95, where the author states that all deliveries to Virginia by the company were shipped on contract with such established merchants in the Chesapeake trade as Jeffrey Jeffreys and Micajah Perry, and that the company made no deliveries on contract to any of the colonies after 1689.

31. Elizabeth Donnan, *Documents Illustrative of the Slave Trade to America* (Washington, 1930–35), IV, 53–55, shows delivery of 120 Africans in 1678 and 177 in 1679. If two vessels reported from Barbados (*ibid.*, I, 250) as having called there on the way to Virginia in the summer of 1679 actually reached their destination with the combined cargoes of 404 Negroes, that year probably brought heavier deliveries by the Royal African Company than did any other year, before or after. There is evidence (*ibid.*, IV, 59–62) that one other vessel, dispatched by the company to Africa in the spring of 1685 under orders to secure a cargo of 190 persons, reached the colony. Very fragmentary evidence has survived to indicate that in 1674 and 1675 the company scheduled four ships for Virginia, but there is no record of deliveries made in documents which do record deliveries to other colonies. See microfilms in Virginia State Library of CO 1/31, f. 32 and of CO 1/34, ff. 109, 110 (Virginia Colonial Records Project Survey Reports 731, 734). That some deliveries at this time may have been made is suggested by Appendix II in Davies, *Royal African Company*, p. 359, which shows Virginia credited with £4,608 in bills of exchange in 1676, the largest such entry for any year.

32. The ship was the *Society* and the surviving record is attributable chiefly to a later attempt by its owners to recover damages. The indexes of H. R. McIlwaine, *Executive Journals of the Council of Colonial Virginia* (Richmond, Va., 1925), Vol. I, and of the *Calendar of State Papers, Colonial, 1689–1692* provide a guide to the rather full record.

33. In addition to Davies, see Leonard W. Labaree, *Royal Instructions to British Colonial Governors, 1670–1776* (New York, 1935), II, 665; and Donnan, *Documents*, IV, 62.

34. Richard L. Morton, *Colonial Virginia* (Chapel Hill, N.C., 1960),

I, 318, 320, 333; Thomas J. Wertenbaker, *Virginia Under the Stuarts* (Princeton, N.J., 1914), p. 254.

35. Lewis C. Gray, *History of Agriculture in the Southern United States to 1860* (Washington, 1933), I, 248–50; Bruce, *Economic History*, I, 350–56; II, 76, 308–12, 314–15; Susie M. Ames, *Studies of the Virginia Eastern Shore in the Seventeenth Century* (Richmond, 1940), pp. 45–49.

36. In addition to the introductory summary in Davies, *Royal African Company*, see J. W. Blake, "The Farm of the Guinea Trade," and R. Porter, "The Crispi Family and the African Trade in the Seventeenth Century," *Journal of African History*, IX (1968), 57–77.

37. Robert P. Brenner, "Commercial Change and Political Conflict: The Merchant Community in Civil War London," (Ph.D. diss. Princeton University, 1970).

38. Nugent, *Cavaliers and Pioneers*, p. 118. The patent listed thirty-seven headrights by name, presumably all white, and the number of Negroes is established by subtraction from the total of sixty headrights.

39. Menefie had gone to England early in the spring of 1637, along with other members of the council, to answer charges by Governor Harvey. See Morton, *Colonial Virginia*, I, 142; *Calendar of State Papers, Colonial, 1574–1660*, p. 256.

40. Bruce, *Economic History*, II, 403; Nugent, *Cavaliers and Pioneers*, p. 120, where the patent gives the names of three different persons from whom the Negroes had been purchased, including a Mr. Constable who may have been Jonathan Constable, a known importer of Virginia tobacco. See Brenner, "Commercial Change and Political Conflict," p. 138n.

41. Curtin, *Atlantic Slave Trade*, p. 55.

42. Nugent, *Cavaliers and Pioneers*, p. 328.

43. *Ibid., Documents Relating to the Colonial History of New York*, (Albany, 1877), XII, 93–94.

44. Ludwell Lee Montague, "Richard Lee, the Emigrant, 1613(?)–1664"; Jacob M. Price, *The Tobacco Adventure to Russia*, in *Transactions of the American Philosophical Society*, n.s., Vol. 51, Pt. 1 (1961), p. 13n; Davies, *Royal African Company*, pp. 295, 383.

45. See in abstracts of Patent Book 8, p. 382, a patent to Joshua Story et al. in 1693 for 185 headrights including 114 Negroes; of Patent Book 9, p. 405, a patent in 1695 to Ralph Wormeley for 270 headrights of which 99 evidently were for Negroes; p. 413, for a patent to William Byrd in 1696 which included 100 Negroes in the total of 113 headrights; and p. 423, for a patent to Bartholomew Fowler in 1698 in which 90 of 130 headrights evidently were for blacks.

46. Hening, *Statutes*, I, 540, which should be read together with I, 469, 536–37, for the legislation is somewhat more complex than the brief statement here suggests.

47. Davies, *Royal African Company*, pp. 299, 363.

48. Donnan, *Documents*, IV, 89.

49. Bruce, *Economic History*, II, 80–84, 317–22, 324–29; Ames, *Studies*

of the Virginia Eastern Shore, pp. 62–65; Arthur P. Middleton, *Tobacco Coast: A Maritime History of Chesapeake Bay in the Colonial Era* (Newport News, Va., 1953), pp. 178ff.; Gray, *History of Agriculture,* I, 209–10; and several references in Harlow's *History of Barbados, 1625–1685* (Oxford, 1926).

50. Middleton, *Tobacco Coast,* pp. 5–6.

51. Davies, *Royal African Company,* pp. 294–95; Donnan, *Documents,* IV, 59; Bruce, *Economic History,* II, 83–84.

52. See especially Curtin, *Atlantic Slave Trade,* pp. 143–44, where he uses data previously drawn from Donnan's *Documents* by Melville J. Herskovits, *The Myth of the Negro Past,* 2d ed. (Boston, 1958), pp. 46–47.

53. See above, p. 35, note 38.

54. In "Epidemiology and the Slave Trade," *Political Science Quarterly,* LXXXIII (1968), 190–216.

55. See, for example, U. B. Phillips, *American Negro Slavery* (New York, 1918), p. 113.

56. One of the additional patents included 23 Negroes, one 19, four 17, and one 16; all others had 9–15.

57. For examples see abstracts of Patent Book 6, pp. 138, 155, and 170, where a total of twelve Negroes were counted in three patents, each granted for one hundred or more headrights.

58. Curtin, *Atlantic Slave Trade,* p. 156. See *ibid.,* pp. 125, 144, and Donnan, *Documents,* I, 94, for evidence that a few of the Negroes brought to Virginia more or less directly from Africa came from Madagascar.

59. See especially Nugent, *Cavaliers and Pioneers,* p. 128, for a patent to Henry Perry which included 12 Negroes, apparently brought from London in 1638, who were purchased by George Menefie from Governor Harvey in 1639.

60. See Greene and Harrington, *American Population,* pp. 136–37, for this and other estimates mentioned, but the date of the pamphlet was 1649, not 1648 as stated there.

61. Davies, *Royal African Company,* p. 300. The instruction was that at least two-thirds of the purchases should be men, but eight or ten boys and girls under fifteen might be included in a shipment if the cost was not high or if there was some advantage "in getting others with them." On p. 299 Davies gives an analysis of sixty thousand slaves actually delivered to the West Indies between 1673 and 1711 which reveals that 51 percent were men, 35 percent women, 9 percent boys, and 4 percent girls.

62. Much more attention has been given the emergence of the large plantation than to the actual distribution of ownership. The best evidence is that offered by Wertenbaker on the distribution of the labor force, white and black, in *The Planters of Colonial Virginia* (Princeton, N.J., 1922), pp. 55–59; see also p. 153 for an indication that well into the eighteenth century the bulk of the slave population was still owned by small planters.

63. For example, see Curtin's discussion in "Epidemiology and the Slave Trade," pp. 213–16; and Edgar J. McManus, *A History of Negro Slavery in New York* (Syracuse, N.Y., 1966), pp. 44–45, 65.

64. But see Winthrop D. Jordan, "American Chiaroscuro: The Status and Definition of Mulattoes in the British Colonies," *William and Mary Quarterly*, 3d ser., XIX (1962), 183–200.

65. *Economic History*, II, 59–60, 107.

66. See again Curtin, "Epidemiology and the Slave Trade"; and for a discussion directed chiefly to disproving the supposition that the earliest settlers in Virginia suffered from malaria, Wyndham B. Blanton, *Medicine in Virginia in the Seventeenth Century* (Richmond, 1930), pp. 50–55.

67. Bruce, *Economic History*, II, 108; *Historical Statistics of the United States, Colonial Times to 1957* (Washington, D.C., 1960), p. 756.

68. Richard Beale Davis, *William Fitzhugh and His Chesapeake World, 1676–1701* (Chapel Hill, N.C., 1963), p. 175; Bruce, *Economic History*, II, 87–92. See also Curtin, *Atlantic Slave Trade*, p. 73, for a comment upon the significance of a natural increase as an early development in the history of slavery in the North American colonies.

69. Thus, Edmund Jennings reported to the Board of Trade in 1708 that there were about 12,000 Negroes in the colony and that importations in the preceding decade came to a total of just over 6,600 (Donnan, *Documents*, IV, 88–90). Neither of these figures may be as exact as one would desire, but there can be no doubt that importations after 1698 became especially heavy. The estimates given in *Historical Statistics*, p. 756, of 23,118 for 1710, 16,390 for 1700, and 9,345 for 1690 indicate that the Negro population grew more slowly in the first decade of the eighteenth century than it had during the 1690s. Such an assumption seems to be extremely doubtful.

INDEX

Brooke Hindle *The Pursuit of Science in Revolutionary America, 1735–1789* N710

Robert V. Hine *California's Utopian Colonies* N678

Preston J. Hubbard *Origins of the TVA: The Muscle Shoals Controversy, 1920–1932* N467

Thomas Jefferson *Notes on the State of Virginia* N647

Rufus Jones *The Quakers in the American Colonies* N356

George F. Kennan *Realities of American Foreign Policy* N320

Gabriel Kolko *Railroads and Regulation, 1877–1916* N531

Howard Roberts Lamar *The Far Southwest, 1846–1912: A Territorial History* N522

William L. Langer *Our Vichy Gamble* N379

Douglas Edward Leach *Flintlock and Tomahawk: New England in King Philip's War* N340

William Letwin, Ed. *A Documentary History of American Economic Policy Since 1789* (Rev. Ed.) N442

Richard P. McCormick *The Second American Party System: Party Formation in the Jacksonian Era* N680

William S. McFeely *Yankee Stepfather: General O. O. Howard and the Freedmen* N537

James Madison *Notes of Debates in the Federal Convention of 1787 Reported by James Madison* N485

C. Peter Magrath *Yazoo: The Case of Fletcher v. Peck* N418

Jackson Turner Main *Political Parties Before the Constitution* N718

Donald R. Matthews *U.S. Senators and Their World* (Rev. Ed.) N679

Burl Noggle *Teapot Dome* N297

Douglass C. North *The Economic Growth of the United States, 1790–1860* N346

Norman Pollack *The Populist Response to Industrial America* N295

Benjamin Quarles *The Negro in the American Revolution* N674

Robert E. Quirk *An Affair of Honor: Woodrow Wilson and the Occupation of Veracruz* N390

Robert E. Quirk *The Mexican Revolution, 1914–1915* N507

Robert V. Remini *Martin Van Buren and the Making of the Democratic Party* N527

Charles R. Ritcheson *Aftermath of Revolution: British Policy Toward the United States, 1783–1795* N553

Eric Robson *The American Revolution, In Its Political and Military Aspects, 1763–1783* N382

Darrett B. Rutman *Winthrop's Boston* N627

Bernard W. Sheehan *Seeds of Extinction: Jeffersonian Philanthropy and the American Indian* N715

James W. Silver *Confederate Morale and Church Propaganda* N422

Abbot E. Smith *Colonists in Bondage: White Servitude and Convict Labor in America, 1607–1776* N592